POPULAR
CULTURE

The Ohio State University Press / *The Journal* Award in Poetry
David Citino, Poetry Editor

1988   Sue Owen   *The Book of Winter*

1987   Robert Cording   *Life-list*

POPULAR
CULTURE

Winner of the 1989
Ohio State University Press/The Journal Award
in Poetry

Albert Goldbarth

Ohio State University Press
Columbus

Library of Congress Cataloging-in-Publication Data

Goldbarth, Albert.
    Popular culture / Albert Goldbarth.
      p. cm.
    "Winner of the 1989 Ohio State University Press/The Journal award in poetry."
    ISBN 0-8142-0498-8 (alk. paper).—ISBN 0-8142-0499-6 (pbk. : alk paper)
    I. title
  PS3557.0354P67   1989
811'.54—dc20   89-32882
                                                          CIP

Printed in the U.S.A.

9 8 7 6 5 4 3 2 1

Acknowledgments

□ □ □

Grants from the National Endowment for the Arts and the John S. Guggenheim Fellowship Foundation have enabled the completion of these poems.

Additionally, these poems have all been previously published in literary journals; appreciation is extended to the editors of

The Beloit Poetry Journal (Shangri-la; The Gulf)

Boulevard (Collecting)

Black Warrior Review (All About)

Cutbank (Powers)

The Georgia Review (By One)

New England Review and Bread Loaf Quarterly (Donald Duck in Danish)

The Ontario Review (Elbee Novelty Company Inc.; The World Trade Center; Qebehseneuf)

Ploughshares (Of the Doubleness)

Poetry (The Multiverse; Again; The Quest for the Source of the Nile)

Thanks to Barbara and David Clewell for their friendship. Thanks to Richard Howard for his enthusiasm.

this book's
for Shnooks

Contents

□ □ □

By One

*And the opinion that every man hath his particular angel may gain
some authority by the relation of St. Peter's miraculous deliverance out
of prison not by many, but by one angel.*

—Izaak Walton

That's all it requires. The law of even
miracles is economy, and one
resourceful angel is all it requires:
a sudden doze upon a warden, the several
molecules of mortar disappearing
from around some stones to the height of a man.
He walked out, into this same night air
that goes at it like a scouring pad
in your lungs and mine. Harsh,
revivifying. And the night sky full
of too much to be familiar. There's a theory
UFO's are the 20th century's angels
—sighted instead of those earlier wonders,
oxidizing the same small heap of needs.
And how many unsleeping nights
has each of us prayed—or whatever version
of prayer is current—for just a single
emissary of one or the other? Not
a battalion, but just one angel, sent
for just one grief that weighs
what each of us weighs, and fills us.
And the sleet falls as if being
background is all that matters. Or
the junebugs whirr, machine-parts
down the lines of night's perspective.
There are times I've walked through darkness
thinking even the hem of an angel would do,
a hem like the northern lights
but personal—sized to my problems.
Just the hand of an angel, just one eddy
on the waters that's the print of an angel's finger.
Just one feather to fall
like snow on my tongue, to enter me like
those sugar cubes of Salk vaccine in the '50s,

small and sweet and metabolic.
Just one feather. Or whatever current
version of a feather is here. One glowing,
silver bolt off a wing. A hinge.
One wheel to steer by.

Donald Duck in Danish

1.

This woman's tongue is being torn out. Yes. And I'm not being
sensational merely to clench your attention. It is, if anything, horribly
matter-of-fact: one Guard-of-Honor grips her hair and the other
saws, two strokes, then pulls. Tomorrow they'll hurt her
sexslit so it grows closed over itself and will never be operable
for pleasure again, will dump her on her doorstep
with their fist-sign burnt to her breast. This poem
can't do a thing about it, can't do one small sprig or whisper
of rescue about it, this or any poem, it hasn't the words. This
poem can say the pizzicati spring rain plays a shingle roof
all day, but it won't help. The deckled edges of antique maps
won't help, the whole ennobled halcyon-to-maggotass wordmastery
this poem can possibly lug to its surface can't heal, although
its empathy is great, although it will not flinch and swears
it won't forget, no, not in its leastmost inky valence,
although it parallels the dark world of that torture room,
touches it, nuzzles, but never penetrates it, like . . . That woman.
Her husband. Years later, in bed. Two bodies so cell-known and
soul-known by each other! Though he can't enter. So known, so
much one—as we say about lovers—they share a common language.

□ □ □

Pizzicati spring rain plays a shingle roof. The Ducks look
out. It clears. They'll soon be whisked from this domestic setting:
Bank Bank Bank is Knock Knock Knock and a door opens
into another adventure. This one, on the High Seas. Oncle Anders
(Uncle Donald) and his nephews, over the dignified deep-blue breves
of waves in comicbook art that must be, on the Ducks' level,
terrible lunges of oceanic pique, or crooks of watery fingers
beckoning islandward. They're following an antique map,
its deckled edges trembling in their tufted glovey hands.
Den naeste morgen, "Land I Sigte!" (*Next morning,* "Land ahoy!")
From then on: pirates, lost doubloons, portcullis-jawed sharks, and
avian Good in battle with rodent Evil until the final panel's SLUT
(THE END). Then more adventures: Tibet, The North Pole. Here,
in Egypt (most exotic *ancient* Egypt, too, through plot-twist trickery)
the plucky Ducks are puzzling at a sphinx's hieroglyphics, which
would "SWOOSH" them magically back in sandy swirls to home, if only
they could read these jackals and ibises. And above them: real
gulls in real sky. And above that: strangely UFO-ish things,
the real eyes of a real Danish reader, who closes her
comicbook slowly then looks up: ducks in high migration, squawking.

□ □ □

It rains, in ancient Egypt. Some. The rest of the sun-drummed
time it's heat that, bad days, makes the greasy edging
of fat along pigmeat froth like a rabid animal. And a man?
Could drag home empty in his spirit, empty-handed,
from the river nets. And a woman. This heat. This shitty little meal
of salt-dried marsh reeds, and this heat. His name is Yuti.
Hers, Taheret. Now, for me, this broken (and mended) red breccia
jar in the shape of a dumb plump duck is something
curatorially attended—labeled, in its cased air. But it isn't
hard to see how it held grain once, or cosmetics, or once, and only
a rage-red moment, was the focus of two people's one day of
absolute ire, was flung, and cracked (and found exactly
with that fracture up its wingline 5 millennia later)—jar
in a world of cobra-hooded hippo-headed deities I'll never read
anything comprehensible into. But I understand that jar.
It isn't hard. The living hands it filled. It isn't hard
because the grief or orgasm-pleasure that make a human face
a dreamy prototype and sweep it to a place above
indigeny, are timeless speech—are everyone's
fatherland's mother tongue. Now Taheret stomps out, mad, muttering.

□ □ □

When I first met Claudia, "Pepe's mom" was "dying"—whoever
Pepe was. At 4 A.M. his *bank!bank!bank!* exploded the sugary
loaf of sleep and sex-exhaustion over the bed, and I was left
in darkness while she murmured him calm in her livingroom, in
their language, from an ongoing story I'd entered mid-plot
and illiterate.—How it always is.—How I must seem, to others.
When I first met Morgan, her sister I couldn't picture was in
a Dallas hospital coughing the mucousy ropes of cystic fibrosis
out of bunched lungs. When I first met Judy, she already owned
that ticket to Japan. Rice paper, green tea, *kanji*, futons. What
we always are is new vocabulary strangers need to learn, to be
less strange, and fluency is a sign of some love or another. That
first morning driving home blur-eyed from Claudia's, I saw
clearly enough, in the pearly unreeling early light and car exhaust,
the carcass of an alleycat was folded as neat as a waiter's linen
over the interstate's guardrail, with a crate of potatoes beside it—one
quick undubbed scene from the foreignest movie imaginable,
though "real life." When Judy left, I read this: "Sweet, my
heart is a maimed dove fluttering."—from the ancient
Egyptian, though true and now and native on my lips.

□ □ □

cockscream heyhelpmeYOWYUMYUM allclawmarks pisssss
the fur-thing fin-and-mane-my-lovely oh wings oh breathing
—Dreaming. Something like Egyptian gods now: the animal
in us risen into, and becoming, the head. Baboon. Hawk. So, in
balance, what's human can rise to the head of an animal: Lucy,
"fastidious, toilet-trained chimpanzee princess," raised her first
11 years in an affluent human family (Oklahoma), learning "about
130 words" in American Sign Language, even compounding her
own: a radish signed as "cry hurt food." On an island
in the blood-warm sluggish Gambia River in Africa (now
that she's large and willful) she's fitfully learning her birthright: how
to be a wild chimp, trap ants, fool snakes, and over time has been
uneducated down to around 20 remnant words I see her
sadly scoring on the shoreline air to no one: "food" . . . "drink"
. . . "Lucy hurt." I think of this de-articulating one morning when
its opposite pulls up: a schoolbus of thirty or more
deaf 5-year-olds, their banter and excited flock of hands,
and someone doing the consuming work of teaching them further
word-stores. Who could live with such labor? I know; and I'll
tell, if only you'll read part 2 of this. My poem. My language.

2.

And I know where we've left the Ducks: perplexed, pith-helmeted,
frustrated—facing a faint inscription, all its persea trees
and cows and asps . . . They have some serum ailing Duckburg
needs: but also have the camel corps of the Rats of Evil
lolloping ever nearer over the dunes and, in the way of menace on this
level, cursing in comicbook esperanto (!**!#!) and spitting (*ptooey!*)
daylong . . . Oh untangle the magic formula, Donald, get your uphackled
pinfeathers out of this jam or pickle or stew or whatever colloquial
Danish calls trouble! . . . In preparation, over years, to decipher
the mystery-glyphed Rosetta Stone, Champollion studied Arabic,
Syrian, Chaldean, Sanskrit, Persian—and a little Chinese grammar text
"for amusement." Donald and company have their Disney Studio
script to rely on, solely, and the very sand seems closing in. She's
followed them, my comics-scanning Danish reader, over those
exotic miles as surely as his "thirteen cheeping mallard ducklings"
followed Konrad Lorenz, that implausibly "imprinted" parent, their own
far waddling way. Again, she closes the book. Again, she goes
to the bedroom. They've had a bad fight. He's sleeping now—her man.
Posed on the sheets. Enigma. Hieroglyph figure. Conversant in worlds,
like all of us, to which, when we wake, we're the deaf and the dumb.

□ □ □

Toes unrinded of bandage for better display, and face the same, so
now her grayish grimace and carrot-red henna coiftop jut
like an ancient surgical blade and its balled-up bloody rag, this
part-ecdysiast mummy lathers us up, as any stripper ought,
for more, and leaves us wanting. "Who *was* she?" There's no real
explanation on her label, and of course the sarcophagus's luscious
wraparound script of knees and waves and lotuses only stymies.
A few cases over, the bones of Jews death's long dismantled are still
awaiting resurrection in their steamer-trunk-sized ossuary boxes
with the writing of my people neatly incised, black pods, black flames.
I'm sorry: I think time won't reflesh that devotional clutter.
I think the closest we may ever come to second life is someone
else's fancy reading the shards of us back to a wholeness. When
I do, I see it's night: the Nile moon's a dazzling platter, and she
brings some of its silver filigree in on her skin, and stands there
staring at her sleeping man—who's on no Danish silks but
on a knuckley hempen pallet, and yet who serves as a translation
for the Danish scene. He wakes and sees her. "I mended it,"
Taheret says. The duck jar in her palms. The moon on fire in her
oranged hair. The glue they make out of their kisses.

□ □ □

Everything's normally peachy in Duckburg. (Even so, they need that
serum.) Once, in Chicago, I listened hard as Gus's oldest girl who was
retarded spoke, her tongue a treadle embellishing out such fine and
faulty lace! But that's here . . . Over there . . . the problem of being
alike or separate also plagues their sages, in the terms of
over there. Just now, the Darwin of Duckburg might be writing: "We
all come from the primordial ink, and a trace of its composition still
informs our bodies. After that, the how and why of who
we are is garbled. Horace Horsecollar is a horse
who rides a horse—that is, Mr. Horsecollar is
a bipedal sentient horse who, in his wingtip shoes,
tweed gadabout slacks and tuxfront-likened horsecollar, can,
when out West tracking ne'er-do-wells with Mickey, ride
pellmell across the sagebrush, on domesticated beasts.
The question of *sapiens:* vexes. The theory of common ancestor stock
survival-of-the-fittest or cosmic rays divided: vexes. Daisy
has Donald over for duck hollandaise; licked fingers. Clarabelle
Cow visits Horace in fieldmouse-gray chichi high heels like gravy boats.
And now his trousers on the floor, and the collar, and now
from the bedroom a pleased and compassionate eloquence of whinnies."

□ □ □

O that you would come to me swiftly, like a horse
of the king's, that cannot be restrained by any chief of grooms
is ancient Egyptian for what I've heard in the buzzed-up wee-hours
mumble between parked Caddies at The Deuces Wild's lot: *oooh*
baby I gon' spread on th' grass fow you, though any lawn was neighborhoods
away from that spot and its jargon. Male porcupines in heat
may spurt their female sweeties with urine from up to 7 feet
as indication of wooing. If I'm confounding love most *haute*
with lust or even simple instinctual mating, or speech
with sign . . . well, still, it's true the universe is little more than layer
on layer of language, often without elucidating
phrasebooks in between. That summer after Morgan's sister died,
she'd call out during sleep, in words the alphabet for which was
crisscrossed hummingbird bones, stone snowflakes, sunspots, DNA. And
Wart the slops-boy, who would one day be King Arthur, you know
was turned by Merlin's wand to a snake, a badger, a kestrel,
a moss-mouthed gar, and later when he needed them their spirits
surrounded his shoulders like smoke that spoke—and each its own
patois and wisdom. Maybe they're around the Ducks now, who this last
split-second succeed in their task, and sandy whirlwinds lift them:

□ □ □

"SWOOSH!" and they're dumped, on their ornithologically-nonexistent
rumps, in real Duckburg, safe, and the serum really delivered
into the Mayor's canine hands. Parades. A sticky kiss from Daisy.
In their better world the best's occurred, and sun sets
down these peaceful streets in maraschino splendor. While
in ours . . . ? In times when "necessary counterproductive numbers" is
a village burnt, a village with its blistered dead
hauled wholesale into the trash wagons, good is never
absolute. Today it's simply this woman, in front of this class.
She can't talk, with her tongue torn from its root, but she can
"talk." That is, can sign. That is, a garnet fist is branded
in her breast-flesh, but her real hands can really open,
splay, twine, buck and fly. It feels good. Her thirty
charges look agog and learn "Vocabulary Drill" without a single fuss
or pee-drenched pair of shorts today, and everything feels good.
The lousy cafeteria tuna lunch is good, the kids do "shoreline birds"
impeccably, and the sky out the window is smooth blue like a square
of drying laundry. There really are days like this. Her husband
picks her up at 5. "So whaddidyou teach the half-pints today?"
The *duck* sign. Then a kiss. SLUT. (THE END.)

Shangri-la

a mystery story

> . . . *forgotten Victorian objects like*
> *the gasogene and the tantalus.*
> —Cait Murphy,
> "The Game's Still Afoot"

1.

People were missing.
Holmes was consulted.
People were being erased like chalk from slate,
in backs of hansom cabs.
Outside, the fresh run of a cloudburst twirled
assorted rinds and papers through the gutters
(Holmes had slept through the rain
but could gauge its intensity easily by the litter's rate)
and an urchin whistling to keep up his spirits
slipped past through the shopfront shadows
(new to the neighborhood, Holmes observed, and
filed away his likeness). Inside,
business as usual. Business, in fact (for him it was always
fact fact fact) was booming: eventually
everyone disappears. And it was simple enough,
the mariner hunkered fetuslike for 3 days
"in a fiendishly clever contraption, Watson: a keg
of pickled cucumbers, so fitted as to enable his being
dryly although uncomfortably housed, with breathing apparatus
concealed in a false stave which I noticed when . . ." But
what of the others? Unnoticeable, and without clues.
"Every night, Mr. Holmes, my wife she
goes to sleep and disappears somewhere beyond our life,
for a good 8 hours. I need to know where!" And
he, who woke alone to see the rainslicked bricks of Baker Street
and always had and always would, was curiously
unfit for such investigation. People were
un-being themselves "in every domicile in London,
Watson, and I am powerless to halt it!"
There were no malefactors, these were only citizens
like you and me. Enter a parlor,
for instance—here's this rage of all the city,

the stereopticon. What it does exactly is take 2 printed images,
2 people, and make them 1. And over time
we can perfect it, we being human and time being time,
can ultra-rarify the principle, and make
1 person no one.
                        At my father's grave
I've often hoped for an answer to this
but there's none to detect.

2.

A woman I know isn't here any more
though she walks and talks with the living. I've seen somebody
rev her Toyota, chug her Bud, whoever it is
it isn't her. She's retreated, she's fled back to that zombie-point
inside a person where all of the lines of the face converge.
An inch? (Maybe an inch.) 100 miles? (The psyche can do that to space.)
Now all of her friends are mourning,
either an inch or 100 miles of mourning, depending on how they perceive it,
and being inside her isn't
sex so much as entering the streets of her skin
at night with the only lantern I have
and calling her name at each crossroads.

□

That afternoon, I worked on my Holmes poem:
words, even the words, were disappearing—all
those "dear" "quaint" Victorian commonplaces
sloughing off the surface of the mother tongue.
Landau clattered by for the last time. *Brougham*
followed close behind. These carriages
vanished on a far rise, leaving only their horses,
bewildered a moment, lightened of the load, then grazing.
They'd never return to an *ostler,* never again. And he
would never cumbersomely buckle into his *ulster.*
Would people seek "lodgings" some time, announcing themselves
by "calling cards"? And what of "jollification,"
what of "apoplexy"—both these bisque-red
flushings of the cheeks were disappearing from the "tradesmen."
I was thinking of a woman I love who
wasn't the woman I love. It was a very old story,
older than we are. Maybe she has "brain-fever."
Maybe I do. Watson has no nostrum
in all of his pharmacopoeia.

□ □ □

That evening, I looked in the mirror.
Really looked. If the face, the actual face-of-the-moment,
is the cross-section
of a conduit the length of a life,
                              then
how irretrievably far back was that 13-year-old
boy in bed with his Dell paperback edition of *The Hound of the Baskervilles,*
living in it
instead of his onerous *bar mitzvah* lessons . . .
On how many hairslicking zitpicking image-attending missions
must he have also languished in front of a mirror, and
still his face remains the most wavery thing for me of all
of 1961.
          My father
stalks to the kitchen for *vishnik*—homemade
blackberry brandy he's sugared to critical mass
in jars about the size of cub plane fuel tanks.
"I-i-i-r-v . . ."—my mother, in her voice
of lyric complaining that says it's half cute, half repulsive
Irv's in full view in his *gottkies,*
his enormous day-stained wholesale cotton underwear.
He dances back to their bedroom with a grackle-purple shotglass of it
for her too. "Hoochie-koo," he croons, relying
on the half that's cute. I hear her: "Check on Albie first."
"A-a-a-lbie . . . You up studying
'Today-I-Am-A-Man'?": his code for the service
I'd need to lead in *shul.* "Uh-huh." That's all
I ever gave them, then: uh-huh, uh-uh: yes, no. They
never understood how much it meant love. And
I didn't either. I'm pouring myself, as lavishly as rosewater
out of a gold bowl into a gem-set chalice, wholly
into the years and miles behind that
cover: the deerstalker hat, the calabash pipe, the magnifying lens
against the best warm umber woodgrain Dell could pay
a hack artist to fake. The pages' edges were
dyed blue: Dell did that in those days. In my skull, a crazy mélange
of "girl groups" must have been contending for attention: the Shangri-las,
the Ronettes, the Angels: they were my first real
image of sex, before I even knew what place in them
my left hand simulated. I remember, clearly,
the lacquerlike cling of the black leather pants on the Shangri-las,
their lacquered apricot asses, when they lip-synched their
"The Leader of the Pack" on *American Bandstand.* I remember . . .
so much. Before all the lights of the house click off,

I'll hear my father creak the hallway floorboards on his way
to check my Grandma Nettie's comfort for the night
—she'd be alive then still, she clung with all her infirm might
to life enough to see her through her only grandson's
Day of Tribal Acceptance. I can see Daddy Irv, now
his face first pushing jowliness, and leaning to kiss her
papery cheek . . . I see it all
                              except for me, the little
kingpin, hinge, incredible burden, income tax deduction, and
jumbled-up joy of their lives. Where am I? I
knock on the mirror—the medicine chest in the bathroom.
It opens. Mrs. Hudson
ushers me in. The mingled scents of nitrate and iodoform compete
for recognition with a fresh gust of the after-rain.
So, yes, he's been experimenting, "the bluish flame of the Bunsen burner"
limning his long gray traveling-cloak,
the Turkish slipper pouched with foul tobacco that he's holding.
"Ah! You've come a long way I see
—from the 20th century." "But, how . . . ?" So
he explains. And why, pray tell, do I disturb the great man?
"It's a matter of direst urgency, I swear.
A 13-year-old boy is missing."

3.

ACD, d. 1930

That afternoon, precisely between
the dray horse and the violin, Holmes
measured the paper, weighed it, clipped
one corner to burn and analyzed the ashes
under chemicals and the glass.
                              That night,
Jean Doyle wrote—her living hand a
glove for a spirit's. Her brother Malcolm
had crossed over. Once his mother appeared
in a seance, gray and vague but "in an
ecstasy of delight." His son Kingsley
had crossed over, now he wrote to them,
through them, in childish scrawl.
And "Phineas" spoke, he was busy "connecting
vibratory lines of seismic power," and that capable spirit
"Walter" rang a bell in a box.
From Yorkshire, there were photographs of real fairies
inches high and gossamer-winged.
A photograph of a medium, collapsed, and
"ectoplasmic matter" drooling in a thick rope
from her nose and sloppily coiling beside her.
The air was loquacious
with stories of "life Over There." In
those days, every pencil
a wooden sill the dead knocked on.
                              "How
could he do it? fairies!—Sherlock's author!"
Elementary. Holmes, that morning,
counted the whorls in a print. Outside,
a hansom passed, and his mind kept track
of its shrill, specific pattern of noise
over cobbles. There was a Queen, her
crown and throne fit—perfect. This many
whorls and this many grams of ash,
Empire, empirical.
                              That dusk,
somewhere hazy before utter dark, Doyle
looked up from his negative of amoeba-like
ghost-glow wafting a manorhouse hallway,
from his photograph of the "psychic cylinder"
manifested when "Margery" turned intense,

from his page: "God's own light must descend
and burn . . ." A black horse somewhere
passed by, or maybe stopped. But Doyle was busy,
believing. A black horse, stopped, maybe
waiting. Something . . . A whiteness, undefinable, could, really
could, appear at the door.
                    "How
could he? *How?*" But how can anyone, and
everyone does. It was 7 July 1930. He saw the
world in which Holmes stood disguised
on Baker Street, the metrics in his head
such a logical outcome the
whole curb shimmied a moment.
The whole street fogged then cleared.
And he crossed over.

□

   a day in the Jimmy Carter years

In these photographs of my father praying
outside, in the yard of the house on Washtenaw Avenue,
in his prayershawl, there's a weight
to his presence, and even to the prescriptual fringe
of the shawl, that the light carries easily

into the camera, and through time. It
makes remembering how heavy the coffin was,
even more difficult. Yes, and it makes the house
seem . . . Do you remember the "neutron bomb" one President
proposed? The people would die. The people

only. Disappear. Yes; but their buildings remain.

4.

The condor only eats meat but can't kill. Relier
on serendipity, it scouts out ground death
daylong, gliding sometimes 40 miles to a feed and 40 back,
so one with air it looks like the unsung mystical pigments
of a thermal have darkened slightly, darkened and ever
so slightly fletched . . . At least, it looks so for the little
time it has left. There are 30 of them, that's all. When these
go, the condor is gone. / But I mean people. For instance,

☐

in 1924 2 Royal Air Force pilots, Stewart and Day,
crashlanded in the Iraqi desert. "Their footprints
were clearly visible in the sand, in an unbroken line
for quite a distance—and then suddenly there were no prints,
not theirs or any others. They were not heard from again."
There are thousands of cases: fresh snow, untrammeled mud . . .
A wife buys a carton of cigarettes and no tobacco ever
Gretels behind her and the rest is silence. / But

☐

I mean only waking up and looking in your eyes
—those zeroes. Only that, as if a simple message had been
typed on a blank sheet, that and that alone. I mean
the blueberry blintzes for breakfast, not the cesareanline
of lightning birthing storm and confusion
into the world, not angels, not the tabloids' fabled
space creatures, no, I only mean being us, touch on touch,
my hand here in your hand that isn't. / But, because

☐

—the eldest—I've shoveled a winter-brittled ritual
first portion of Chicago dirt on my father's lowered casket,
heard it thud against the door of wherever
he was now, I know yours isn't death, not really.
Call it almost-death. In bed I look up. You're
beside me, and I look up. It's dark. I see a dark circling.
I imagine it's the ceiling fan. Midsummer and
it's the ceiling fan, though I call it almost-condors.

5.

Well now I'm thrice thirteen.

In 1961—on September 3rd of that year—the last of the first-run segments of *Rocky and His Friends* was aired. That plucky derringdo cartoon flying squirrel (remember? in aviator goggles) and his humongous-hearted oaf-brained chum, cartoon moose Bullwinkle J. Their spinoff *The Bullwinkle Show* premiered just 3 weeks later, September 24—early Sunday evening (I believe opposite, or was it following, *Lassie*) in attempt to lure a slightly more adult audience with the twosome's droll self-referential antics. ("What NOW, Bullwinkle?" "I dunno, Rock—*shrug*—I haven't read th' script.")—That last in Bullwinkle's half-hollow dippity voice. "I have the best job in the world," said Bill Scott in an interview: the moose's voice for all of the moose's years (plus the voice of Mr. Peabody, mild-mannered dog scientist, and Dudley Do-Right, Mountie).

They were a must for me in those days, and I know where they are today: in reruns. 39, and I can still tune in with fresh glee to the adventure with the moonmen Cloide and Gidney, or the search for the anti-gravity metal Upsidaisium. Where Bill Scott is, though, is more problematic. He died on Friday, November 29, 1985—"survived by his wife, Dorothy, two sons and a daughter" and all of that canned enthusiasm of Bullwinkle J.'s at the weekly manual launching: "Hey Rock: alley-OOOOOP!" And somebody somewhere knows the fate of the Shangri-las, as somebody knows which of the cold stones on the face of Earth once flew through the heavens on fire. And Grandma Nettie, now? The *bar mitzvah* was a success. If you don't believe me, I have photographs. Everyone's smiling. And then she died. I remember my father mottled by afternoon light where he stood alone at the lace-draped windows, staring out at the infinity-point and asking in a low voice, *why?* Well I knew why. She'd seen her grandson *bar mitzvahed* and then that life-support apparatus was unplugged.

And that boy? Where is *he* now? Here, I guess you could say, writing this. But where did he go each night for an hour before sleep claimed him? There might be a moment: his father glides by: the boy he loves so much is translucent, ghostly, soaked

in

to the rained-on page
where London streets
extend through the gaslit blackness.
Yes, and soaked to the skin.
But then, his clothes are barely slop-cart rags.
And even so, he's whistling—some
to fake a kind of grownup nonchalance,
but also some from pure high spirits.
Across the way and above,
Holmes peers out the window and takes impeccable note

21

of his neighborhood's newly-acquired urchin:
perhaps he can be of use some time
on a case—intrigue and danger!
Then the famed prognosticator turns away
to business—Mrs. Hudson has just admitted
a strangely-attired 35- no, 39-year-old
client into his chambers.
The boy, meanwhile, walks on. He
isn't even me by now. Let's say
I was elsewhere.
Let's say the boy kicked stones all the way
to a tidily-tended neighborhood,
shopkeepers' modest houses.
He was a little chilly by now but
adventureful enough not to mind.
He looked in a window, a beckoning
amber opening in the dark. We
didn't see him, busy with sorrow and love.
You were playing a tune on the gasogene,
I was fitting the heirloom tantalus over my head
for the last time in history.

All About

We need to know about somebody worse than we are
turning better. Then there's hope for us. So one night
in the rockbottom 30's a boy sits with his whole self
being beamed up the waves of the radio. Little
Orphan Annie. At least, he has parents. She
came attachless into this breakspirit world. And then
the relentless adventures: in a gypsy circus,
outwitting racketeers, defending the lame boy.
Miss Asthma was mean. Uriah Gudge was positively
despotic. The Asp and Punjab were allies. The original
comicstrip version is built in fleecy loops
and deeply inky hachure that polarize moments of ease
and moments of burden, fracas, and outright menace.
Though she has—"pluck" is what they call it. She
toughs it out, she cuts the grease, she sows and sudses.
She's exactly what America needs, of course. It's 1933:
the painful waiting faces in soup-dole lines grow thinner
yet more numerous (a nasty way for fate to keep stability)
and real babies are really found, rag-wrapped, in real
ashcans: this, he lifts off the news. That night he hears them
argue. Money. At least, he *thinks* they're his parents.
Though in the yard, the sky with its component emptiness
and flamings says that origin is mysterious, and meant to be;
and the future, obscure; and it asks the Insomniac Questions: why
does *anything* happen? is it enough, to be good? what *is*
"good," anyway? . . . Well, he tries. Last Tuesday Chandler
Dupree, the corner's singing shoeshine boy, disappeared
"without a trace" is how they say it, and he's searched the town
all week with his Little Orphan Annie 3-Way Power Telescope
he sent for with a dozen coupons saved from that shit-icky cereal.

□ □ □

We've seen those photos and now it isn't enough. We've
seen the hunger-chiseled faces of Okie farmers like those
on Easter Island: long, stone, imperturbable. It won't do.
In their dustbowl-dun emulsifier colors, it isn't enough.
Go in. Put sand on your tongue. Let that
be a country road going nowhere. And a girl's been walking it
too many days. Go in. I don't mean sex. Go in her, easy,
deep. Go hand over hand down the sinewy cables
of deprivation swaying in their dark shaft. I mean want is something
alive here, it will crawl across your cheek in the night. Just
her size. Your size. Furry and cool. I mean this girl
a landscape. In a wonderful book by George S. Chappell, *Through
the Alimentary Canal With Gun and Camera,* a party of crazed
pith-helmeted explorers "do" a human cavity, vast, expansive,
an Africa: the Sokol illustrations show our body's tubes
like logmill sluices, all of the *sapiens* sweetbreads spread
like hillock and veldt. But that was funny, and 1930. Now
I mean a few years later. Open that lavish coffeetable book
of Great Depression photos: riots; viaduct 'bo camps; mostly
faces staring like rows of cheesecloth masks. In a tent
a preacher's buying an audience with the promise of donuts.
Hell makes him hot, and he's working up Hell, and sweat
as thick as a pomade coats his gray skin. Everyone else
just stares. They're gray too. Black and white have lost
their energy, and dissipated to this sad middle range.
The flap's half-open. Outside, sun hits like a shovel.
A sandlined country road winds by, and a girl is
trekking it, whistling, chipper almost. Her name
is Annie. The dog beside her says *Arf!* in his little balloon.

□ □ □

But Chandler Dupree of the magic black wax and soulful soprano
is vamoosed for good. A week of fruitless detectiving, and
the telescope, despite all of its Powers, gets dropped in the box
with last year's Captain Comet Secret Decoder Ring
and a Junior G-Man Flashlight. In a month, his Mom
will bundle them up for the Goodwill truck, along with her own
dream fodder—what his Dad looks up from his sports page
at, and calls "that Hollywood hokum." Bunk. Malarkey.
Today, malarkey of an especially meaningful sort: Lucette
Retallio, who a very drear 2 years ago sacked 'taters
at the local Buy-Wise Grocery, with her oceanically-moody
18-year-old's eyes providing the neighborhood's only true
exoticism, today plays icy-hearted femmes fatales in a chain
of movie swoon-and-sobbers; and her story "exactly
as told to our reporter," from her discovery snugging the cereal
next to the fresh corn, to her draped-with-diamonds starlet
coronation, is headline-ballyhooed FROM BAGS TO BITCHES
in cover type that's nailpolish red. His mother reads it, in
her sink-stained dollar apron, transfixed. And he . . . He
stares unconvinced at his breakfast cereal. *This* crapgoop
he eats for coupons' sake, a link to some celebrity's past?
And that's the least of his questions. For instance, when
does "the future" begin? Day and night revolve in each other
over the planet like two hands trying to wash
a film of Eternity off themselves. What does it mean, what
does it all mean? Time is painfully mysterious. First
the truck rumbles off with its cargo of donated junk and
now, before you even realize it, it's 1987. Today
that telescope in mint condition is catalogued (I've seen it) at
$150—what America is all about.

□ □ □

So: Little Orphan Annie, and her pupilless blancmange
eyes. And Little Annie Rooney, too—she was a copycat comicstrip
runaway waif, whose daily derringdo premiered in 1927, 3 years
after her namesake's first urchinesque appearance. Rooney's
dog was Zero, not Sandy, and she said "Glorioski!" instead
of "Leapin' lizards!" Each had her fans. In England, someone called
Belinda Blue Eyes searched the world for her Daddy every day.
Buck Rogers searched planets. Tarzan defined liana
parabolas from jungle tree to tree. There is no end to needing these
escape personae. Even now the phone rings: Sid M
saying the medics opened up Ambrose finding impossible
bodymush instead of an esophagus, and in this silence
Sid and I are telling each other we don't want to be on Earth,
in our skins, to face it. What will Mary do, and the kids?
Or Leigh—whose daughter tried to pill herself to death,
was institutionalized, and there ransacked the pharmacy for
more of the same—what shitty little comfort can I give her over
lunch? The jungle warlords dig a trap for Tarzan, leaves
rigged over a pit: and I think of my friend J trying
to sleep tonight, he'll hit the deceptive sheets then fall
through 8 hours of horrible dark . . . So many Great
Depressions! As many as people, I think. There is no end
to needing a personal version of Annie's balming patois:
Don't you worry. Everything'll be jake someday. 6
million listeners tuned in to her radio brio daily.
The strip was carried by 500 newspapers. "In those
vacant eyes is a touch of genius—any reader can place his
chosen expression there. To that extent, the stalwart
Annie is Everyman." And Buck is flushing badguys from
some Martian woods with expertise oncology units just dream of.

□ □ □

Now he's an archeologist—a famous old sot. That first time
at his mother's grave, as they lowered it down perfunctorily
like a steelmill ingot, he couldn't help thinking how strange,
for once, to be putting bones *into* the planet. Though one day many
years later, scapulae in a display case, gleaming white
and wide as wings, say our ideas of museums and Heaven are
one—for both are a saving. And he *does* save!—pennies
in juice jugs, scrap foil, strings, stamps. When you're 10
in the Depression, it leaves its mark. It's not a thriftiness
so much as it's a love: he'll spend cash wildly
in "junktique shops" reclaiming the stuffs of his youth: The Sacred Scarab
Luck Ring, The Sky Commando Photomatic Code-o-graph Badge,
the Flip and Her Buddies Milk Mug . . . In a dustclumped auctionhouse
one day he finds himself bidding with manic abandon, and
leaves with it carried like a jeweled scepter: whatever 3
"Powers" its lenses supposedly had (it never really worked) it
has a 4th now: he can see his past. He can stare at it
firmly and, with no sifter or shovel, his past rises up:
the tongue-scourge taste of that cereal . . . how his father's
addled brain gave up, in those last months, after the surgery . . .
And the questions that he asked at 10 are still the questions
now: below the stars some nights, he wants to know, still:
how come we bear their names, their genes, and anyway
feel orphaned? where does it go, when it stops? what
is it in us, that moves when we sense that the night moves?
where do "solid objects" end? and—what's it all about?
He's 64 now; what's it all about? He remembers, maybe 30
years ago, hearing the tv emcee shout: "Now a big hand for Chandler
Dee and the Shines!"—great a cappella—applause. One mystery
solved. What America, in any case, is all about.

The Multiverse

1.
As a ship, in sinking, sucks whatever flotsam
fills the widening mouth of the cone of its disappearing,
under with it (a liner even taking small boats): so,
of course, a space ship x'ing into hyperspace takes
everything in a certain range of the skin of this universe
with it, to that otherskin: and people have popped from sight,
and even planets: this is simply a fact. The fiction is
in description: a thousand raygun-crowded novels I read
at 16 inside-out'ed the continuum between
one step and another: and someone walks unknowingly into an
Else Dimension: then knows it: the sky is broccoli-green;
the people, sparsely downed all over their bodies, with plumage
in intimate folds; and they project their psyches
corporeally in times of distress, so warring with yourself is a matter
of actual bludgeons and scimitars. There are nurseries with
the crystal eggs of those people in chandelier-sized cairns; and clan
and clan in battle; and gender and gender under the double moons.
You close those books and set-scenes from the real Earth
we're born on gleam like keys to converse worlds: a stack
of yakbutter patties; the hellish, leaping tulip of fire caged in a
steamship's boiler room; two smoky ponies pacing
with the shade a billboard circles through a field on an August day . . .
In ancient Egypt, standing at the doorway to the Afterlife meant
weighing your heart on a scales, against the Feather of Truth.
And haven't I slept with my head on a bag of many
such feathers, nightly, tossing, under a weight . . . It could be
every time we wake, a space ship's bobbed us back from 8
black hours in a parallel plane of the multiverse, and
if not, it's as good a story as any, and true this way: for us,
though space is stable, time is a current. Its ocean is hypertime.

2.

But I was 8, with my ear to the door. Time
didn't exist; I mean that exactly. Remember 8?—a
single continuous atoms-width slip of the present always
encases you: the way a glaze of "breathable" carbon dioxide holds
each plantlike "man" of the far starsystem Kívatoo in an environment
precisely his size and shape. Or, like the Hopi: here,
in mesa light, on the sandstone cliffs, near the 40-feet-deep
rush of the arroyo washes, there is no word for time; there is
no tense to verbs, and seasons aren't nouns, but conditions
of being; and when the gods return from the mountains
to the world of the sandy-floored vulvular arroyos, Oraibo,
Weepo, Polacca, Dinnebito, we know we're in a cosmos-seam
congruent with our own, or interpenetrable with our own, but
not our own by any imaginable means.—What William Herschel
might have felt, discovering infrared: suddenly another planet
occurred on our planet. He might have known, at the end of it all,
in empirical, corseted, regulatory 19th-century London, in
a single overpowering blow so strong it erased all trace of itself
from his mind: the designs of a flower's petals
are landing patterns for bees; yes there are perfectly 3-dimensional
mountains and valleys of sound, to the bat; and over C
are musics hounds can hear the way a saint sees angels higher
overhead than the sky goes. Or: my ear
was to the door. I heard them, Auntie Regina was mixing up
her words. She said she'd ride the stove to the doctors and Mommy
cried at that. Daddy tried to soothe. And there were other words in this
opaque and untranslatable adult-level powwow: cancer,
brainscan, beneficiary. Only the terror came through.
How thick is a door? an inch? But the elders of the tribe were speaking
the High Tongue. They could have been lightyears away.

3.

Cheyenne was raised by Indians—Cheyenne Bodie, of
the tv show *Cheyenne,* who "turned out with the
best traits of two worlds"—weekly. I was 8 in 1956 and Cheyenne was,
I thought, timeless: Doer of Good, and Wooer of buckskin-skirted
Almost-Goods with their wickedsweet dancehall eyes. In this one
he rescues a blonde-braid beauty strapped to a Pawnee pony
by calling at it *halt* in "Injun lingo"—*heenya ho!* The theme music
lifted my life pipette-wise into its veins, and then enlarged me
in its heart: for an hour my own small hopes expanded to the level
of the Winning of the West. But it was science-fiction novels
by 16—hey, remember 16?—your past, an embarrassment; your future,
so long off you'll never twice-16 the way you twiced-8
overnight, without trying. So escape: in this one, Kívatoo
clanwarriors are massed against the Birdfolk, with
those terrifying bioguns that fire the enemy instantly (but
are powered by the user's mind, so every blast shortcircuits out
a memory from his neural record)—and only an Earthman
realm-routed here in search of a kidnapped Federation Princess
can save them . . . I put down the book. Outside,
the streets I've known for 16 years are tarred and gem-set
by the billion shells and greenblack blood of a summer plague
of beetles. It's like oil slick and the highways are shut.
Air whirrs like a part in a giant machine. It's
Boschian (though I don't know the word), it's surely another
galaxy's art or ecosphere or nightmare overlaid like a stencil
on Northside Chicago. Across the street, on their screened-in porch,
the neighbor couple touches in an easy sexuality I can't
imagine although I've dreamed her. He must be 32. She
strokes him, farther from me than the moon. I'll never project myself
into his labyrinth head, or her rosefoliate secrets.

The Gulf

"Smilin' Mighty Jesus!"
She smiled, too. She held her baby
to the specialist like a small black bag
of priceless goods—which it was, of course,
in a way—and said her village doctor said
"my girl gots Smilin' Mighty Jesus,
yessuh, praise the Lord!"

1.

At a certain place, in a certain season, and with
a serendipitous constellating of their chemical flux,
the diatoms glow
in mild winking patches, and this
diluvian sequinning gives a faery surface
to the waters of the gulf. If you enter
and dunk, then rise, you'll also be a source
of light—against the night
it might even seem your body is intensifying
that power, as if sparkage occurs
when blood and ocean call each other
wildly, in a special electrolytic lust,
across the massive, negligible, utterly mysterious
width of human skin.
I've seen it—off a 4-corner bungalowed beach town
in between Corpus and Galveston. All that
glowing, all that giving up of yourself
to the wash of the genesis-mixture about you . . .
Oh—and
there are sharks. One night, a 19-year-old woman
on the concrete apron feeding into the jetty,
kidneys ripped. I walked up
after the crowd but before the medics.
Even in pain and opened up monstrously,
wrongly, even become an ivory locker of meat,
with death sucking fast at her lips, those
starlet good looks gave her
otherwise tragic dishevelment
an intimate, peepshow attractiveness—so
the faces of strangers circling her established every

partum of reaction, from an empathetic, keening grief,
to something more like voyeuristic pleasure or,
on the face of the teenage retarded boy, a something
like seeing a longtime-worshiped goddess
grabbed obscenely down to the level of mortal affairs.
An elderly woman gags. Some guy in back
toys suspiciously with his pocket. Maybe 20 of us.
It lightninged once—we jumped like a single animal.
For all our differences, equally plugged in.
As if she were an organ, pooled in nutrient, and
we were feeding similarly off her,
through our respective invisible tubes. I think I've never seen
such disparate people so close before or since.
And then we'll read, next day, she lives; her fiancé
donates a kidney. For a minute
it will know the focused incandescence of surgical light
on its paleozoic bean-sleek sides—the only
light that it will ever know—and then
be sewn inside a new dark. Then the papers will lose
all interest in them. They'll marry. They'll have a
decade of papers delivered. One night he'll
walk the beach, beclouded, remembering spurts of when
he made his decision and let them cut in.
He's never been that close to her again. That ounce of him,
kissing her blood . . . He's never been that close to her.

2.

It lightninged once.
(A beautifully emphatic gash, by
Kenneth Strickfaden, king of Hollywood's "Edison medicine.")
500 people in one galvanic jerk, and then we
each lapse back to a tight black capsule
of moviehouse isolation. Karloff
wears his 40 lbs. of makeup and costuming like the
curse it is—each lurch:
a penance; every successfully-rendered
gesture (lifting a beaker, shading his eyes
from slatted sun): a cause for wonder so primary, so
very obviously without a remembered history of beakers or shade,
it's near-australopithecinely pure. If you
know only the cheap gore-larded sequels . . . These
two originals done in '31 and '35 by director James Whale
are immensely sympathetic, if moody,
studies of alienation. In the creature's eyes, we see
the pain of internal organs
expatriate from their congenital bodies, trying
to work, to speak a common language, but
dissolving, like world powers in congress, horribly
into clumsy lunges and misfires. He's a sack
of little chasms, held by scarstitches
so thick they look like rungs—and weeping's as appropriate
as terror. Finally, the chasms are externalized.
He's given a bride, his own kind: lab
fleshpatchwork. I know 500 people have watched
his awkward attempts to touch her
—all right-angle stumbles—with 500
separate, perfect understandings. It's
hopeless of course. She's repulsed by him too.
With her grizzlepiles of hair and swatched skin,
with her morgue-filched innards, she's
repulsed by him too. And I can swear at least one
teenager in that ommateum of 500 pairs of eyes
cried at the unbreachable distances people live
inside of, cried despite the horror-genre pyrohyperbolics,
all the walk home from the 1200 block of Division
where the Division Theater spent the last of its
old-time marquee flash, up the stairs, to his room,
from his immeasurably everyday reasons of silence and rejection,
cried immeasurably . . . (If he told you his story
of longing for the nightshift Quick-Pick checkout girl . . . ! But

really, you'd be bored.) So why
remember it now?—the woman tonight an opened treatise
on disconnection, staining the jetty? this
sudden sky-splitting bolt? that
I'm vacationing these thousand miles away from you
for mutual respite? but phone you anyway? something
in the tragedy tonight encouraging sewing back
the small ripped seams of marriage? remember
that night in my office? don't hang up! remember the first
lovetussles? being parts of something
larger we gave breath to, monstrous or not?
together? remember? hello?

3.

It's not only that her body was perfect.
Every concentration-line or shift of her bearing bespoke
another realm, of Ideal Forms. But also,
her body was perfect. And he'd been adoring her now every day
all summer—the retarded boy.
—Who was raised in the Home like one more potato
unloaded into the bin.
—Who was told: With soap, behind your ears
and between your toes. Be quiet. Speak up.
If a policeman stops you, right away
show him the card in your wallet.
—Who washed. Who was quiet. Who spoke up.
—Who was shaved like a sheep once a month.
—Who knew what he meant. Who spoke what he meant like a mouth
at the other end of the universe.
—Who never had a visitor. Who turned 16 without visitors.
—Who saw her in her tangerine bikini on a lime towel.
(She was a shout for the eyes.)
—Who every day returned and every night his dream was
this: that he would die for her if needed, and a hundred years from now
they'd meet in Heaven and be in love.
—Who lived for her. Who saw her
dragged from the waters one night like a net of bloody meat.
—And the crowd. And the ambulance. And the police.
And obscenely, a carnival excitement.
His goddess. Photographers. Sirens.
—Who ran to the Hanskie Bridge in the middle of town
and cried to God from the rail. All night.
—Who was a shabby, babbling figure.
Get the police. / They're down by the jetty. / I'll go.
—Who bayed like a hound.
—Who died in his grief.
—Who was shot to death through the chest
by the police, who said "We told him to stop
and raise his hands or we'd shoot."
—Who was retarded, 16, and confused.
"We saw him go for a gun."
—Who'd reached (in strict obedience,
the only language he knew) for the card in his wallet,
just as he'd always been told.

4.

". . . the lightning flashed along the coast"—this
is from Trelawny's account—and at daybreak he
continues searching for Shelley, who is "on his way home
in the Gulf of Spezia." This is now Tuesday,
the 9th of July, 1822. We know about the corpse
he finds, "the face and hands . . . were fleshless."
And we can guess at the immoderate distress
of Mary Shelley; as if the death of her mother
10 days after childbirth; and that ever-receding
interest of the dispassionate father; and Fanny's
laudanum suicide; and Harriet's
drowning suicide; and the death of her own first
daughter "less than two weeks, only"; and Willy
gone, and Clara gone, reduced to two already
lusterless locks in an album—weren't enough.
So now the Gulf took
him, too. No wonder she needed retreating,
no wonder Trelawny once joked they should seat her
at table "to ice the wine." So now
she's walking that shore like the only human being
left, the heavens clenching
vapor into small gray threatening fists,
her husband's manuscripts in ribbons in the trunk,
his last remaining
flesh in ashes . . . But
                    it's possible to see her
6 years earlier—19, and by a friendlier water,
the shores of Lake Leman, her evening walks with him there
through a light Swiss air so intimate and lucid,
normal thought seemed a kind of clairvoyance, and
with the other two as well, Polidori & Byron, bits of memory
(a pumpkin one of them boated in from God-knows-where,
a nacre-throated mandolin, ghost stories, German beer): these
flock like birds about their figures now and roost
in random order, often accompanied by the lake's own
metronome lapping, and something of standing with him
in the columns of their Villa while the rising sun
gave a marmalade-glaze to the water and his hand went
spidery first, then hungrily, over her unlaced breasts . . . And
here, for once at least in relative belonging, is where
she makes first notes on her "orphan
of science," the "horrid thing," although it knows
Paradise Lost and can read and write French

(the movies ignore this), outcast, bag of plagiarized organs,
"filthy mass that moved and talked,"
and the two of them, up the whole night,
                                        loving. I
don't know if it sufficed.—And don't know what
abiding strength
a time of vital commonality provides, against
the decimating powers. Maybe little. But it's all
we can do, so should do—she did. Whatever it meant,
she had it, long before she had that other thing
Trelawny snatched last-minute from the crematory fires,
and later presented to her: the entire heart,

□

is what I say, or a more coherent version of what I say,
long distance / *don't hang up* / a boardwalk phone
with thunder and ambulance-flash in the background
showing me the "yes" that we *can* say, we *should*—because
the world is storing "no" on "no" for use against us.
There are teeth in the water below its gentle glow.
There are bone-splitting blasts sky stacks in its sweet blue atoms.
I'd start driving back right now if you wanted.
Hello? I'd start driving back right now if you wanted. Hello?
The line a thousand miles long. Hello?
/ *this static* / Hello?

□

is what I say, or a version of what I say, in poems
—this poem. The line a thousand miles insular. Yes.
This poem: as if it mattered. This poem: the static.
Shouting *Mary Shelley! Percy Bysshe Shelley!*
Richard Hugo: "If you went down to the supermarket, and screamed
'Wallace Stevens!' all they'd do is
call the cops." Yes. Not that Stevens cared to hear
the checkout girl's empassioned banal sob stories.
Hello? This static, this line. This telephone wire
as black as the night, with its lightning
allowing our voices. So thin.
So much. As if it mattered. I'd start driving back right
now if you wanted. A thousand miles. We've all been abandoned
in places on Earth where custom is separate from custom,
speech divided from speech, a person kept from people,
by traditional colors, or callings, a marker, a border, a mound,
the offcenter sound of a neighboring accent, a gate latch,
some trickle the width of a wrist.

Spinal meningitis. But
they figured that out
too late. And we call it a single
English language! The baby was buried
in a plain slat coffin about the size of a tool chest,
where the family's always buried its dead,
a plot of saltshot, cantankerous dirt
under sea-wind that blows without end
from the gulf.

Of the Doubleness

(BA-LAM!) "They're coming in from close to 12 o'clock!" (by
which was meant not time but running out of time)
"Well this is for that Axis stooge and his boss The Scarlet
Claw!" (ackackack: gunner fire) "They've blasted me,
Captain Miii . . ." (the fading out of a sturdy Midwestern voice)
"You're not a goner yet, Scotty" (an even sturdier voice) "not
while America cheers us on, and The Secret Squadron is airborne!"
Then Ovaltine peddled its wares, and then the nightly code
for over-and-out. Then some program that bored him
—the Professors of Swingology were scaling a ladder
of jazzy licks up the night sky. Then upstairs: bedtime. He
was alone now with his square of window and Secret Squadron
blackout paper, in case he was needed to shield his portion
of Kyle, Texas from enemies out in the vast star-banded grandeur.

□ □ □

Downstairs, they made love—the famous "two-backed beast,"
their try to sew the halves of Plato's crazy origin-hermaphrodite
happily whole again . . . She wished her mind would shut
the fuck up sometimes! Yes, and let the body simply ride its crests . . .
But even coming, she was thinking. *Sssh* (to herself) *or*
Robbie'll hear. And there was the brother her boy was named for,
he would only say he was shipping away on "Army business,"
just that, and with Nazis like on the radio conquering Europe . . .
Sex's residue is fond and otherworldly. When her flush cooled,
she walked naked and slow through the dark rooms. Well,
not total dark. The moon grew poignant golem-life
in vases, chairs, the scrap tin from their yard—the souls of her sleeping
son and husband filled this milky light . . . Why was it "pathetic,"
or a "fallacy," how her life could be doubled by objects?

□ □ □

It was midnight. It was 1942 and it was midnight and
he sat up in bed—he thought how he was 12 and so
was the clock. Outside: the neighborhood houses, the moon.
And somewhere even beyond the moon: the War. There's this
about a war—like anything else, it's a product
that's sold. It's money for someone. It's always money for someone, and
for someone else it's sitting all night in a hole of your own
sick shit and a thin black trickle of your copilot's brains,
all night, until the strafing stops, and sun lights up
the worms out your ass. It's that. And it's this: it's bought.
He'd met his friends at Osborne's Five and Dime. They gave the secret
Captain Midnight handshake. Nothing's truer than this, or
sweeter: all day they'd searched the streets of Kyle, Texas for spies
of The Claw's. They saved scrap metal. They said their prayers.

□ □ □

Herr Professor. Of mining and engineering. U of Texas
degree. And then he worked for Germany, forwarding drawings
of Allied line deployments to an agent called "The *Schwanz.*" And
even deeper than that, and beyond, he worked for Washington.
His "Army business." Robert Shefthall, double agent, dead now
in a lump of his guts in France, found out, shot down, by Jerry
antiaircraft ackack. Dead with a best friend's brains
caked intimately to his body. "The *Schwanz*": "The Prick." Not
like The Claw at all at all. And he was no
what's-his-name, the hero, Captain Miii . . . then darkness
fills an upturned helmet like a bucket of currant jelly,
though no one's alive to see it. / Though he's my fiction. I
say Robert Shefthall lives. I offer you this alternative
version: the prayers of his nephew save him.

□ □ □

and please keep Uncle Robert alive. The sky leaned down:
"He's not a goner yet." I say Resistance fighters,
cindersmeared to blend with the night, compartmented him
in a freshly-clubbed eviscerated cow, and brought him
breathing to their clinic. Okay, I don't believe it
completely myself. But stranger stories than that came home
from the War. A tale of one twin waking screaming when the other
twin was bombed—transoceanic ESP, its un(-explain & -deni)able
tie and viability . . . dozens of cases. Or Kyle, Texas:
their top ob.gyn. man joined the underground in France.
However they broke the news to Robbie, it was this: his baby
sister died at birth. Whatever it meant to him, that Other he
has and doesn't have, his Secret Squadron of one, will visit him
all through his life. He's 12, she's 0, he whispers to her.

□ □ □

It was midnight. He woke, some dream . . . *a cow around him,*
gunfire, theme music . . . fading already. Noises from
downstairs. "Sssh" (to his absence-of-sister) "they'll hear us."
He thought, he hoped, it might be thugs of The Scarlet Claw's.
But sometimes the War, all ration stamps and insignia patches,
lost its root in this universe and floated off to nothing. It
was 1942. His parents, fallen down a chute of moon
to the livingroom carpet, loving. His first abrasive awakening
peek. And, muted, a 78—"Swingology Hour"—oohing
off the Victrola. He tiptoed back. He knew it frightening but
magic, to have seen this clumsy, pasty-blanch enactment of his own
chromosomal first moment, in their huff and cleave. Not
that he thought of it in those words; but there it was, one
creature, who were two in the clear Kyle everyday noon.

Again

There was such darkness in him then. And I repeated,
at the bedside, something—what, I don't remember exactly but
something simple, something with the desperate hope we find
inside ourselves at times like that, it might have been only
don't let him die incanted until it transcended being
words, or even prayer, but was a relegation of breath to that preliterate
place faith comes from—something meant to be a chain or list
of small lights through his darkness. So I thought of Japan,

the *Sheet of 1,000 Buddhas:* how a single woodblock stamp has meant
so many duplications of the same small holy figure—each,
its nimbus; each, its dole of glow to keep back its commensurate
dole of benightedness. They finally make a pattern each is
lost in: each a quantum of light, in light. In fact in 770 A.D.,
the Empress Koken commanded one *million* prints of a Buddhist charm
be stamped by copper blocks, "to ward off illness" says the story, which is
this story as well. And if I digress right now to the story

of Chunosuke Matsuyama who, in 1784, wrecked half-dead on a coral reef
with 43 others, scratched his story of woe and goodbye on wood and
slipped it with ritual into a bottle, then the bottle in the swift Pacific drift . . .
it doesn't mean I've forgotten that hospital bed, my father
dwindling in it, or the mission of this poem. But
there's a bottle, under sun and over sunfish, blue in cerulean waters,
jet in black, and later I'll return to it. Repetition is what
this poem is about, repetition is what this poem is about.

□ □ □

Even in the oldest stories, it's always 3 wishes, always
3 importunate *open sesames* at the lamp cache's sandstone door.
Luck thrives on serial attempt: perhaps because luck knows how
failure comes first. The ploughboy in the Japanese fairy tale
needs succeeding at 3 tasks (make fire from water,
etc.) before he's awarded the princess's hand. But oh,
time is longer than fortune, my dearests, my sweet ones.
Read the wedding banns 3 times and thrice fling rice, yet

I've seen Jimbo's marriage undo one dawn like a sparrow
their tom brought, head half-hinged and brains sopping out, with
delicacy to their doorstep. Nothing assures. One night
I opened the door on my wife in a terrible, naked parallelogram
of streetlight on the bedsheets—nearly crushed by the light,
so weak she was then, and crying into her hands and God's ear
why me why me why me: and I understood that 3-time cry
reversed us back to zero. Even so, we try; in the face

of everything shaking its great head *no,* we try
to hold on to whatever little over-and-over-again shapes
methodology from nothing . . . The nightshift nurse. I'd
watch her smooth the bed or sometimes his forehead
past smoothness, and into a level of ceremony
purely. —20 shakes of the thermometer. And 19 of them
unnecessary—unless needing wishing is necessary. Just
one rub at the genie's lantern never efficacious.

□ □ □

Of course I visited. And my sister. My mother
kept absolute vigil. And even so, I know he was alone
inside the tubes. I know I'd stand there trying to think myself
immeasurably into the cells, the sick ones, down the fundament of what
we are, to where it all begins, and by such empathetic thinking
burnish the blastula of him clean . . . But no, the tubes, the tubes
are insular. Pain is insular. And the glaze across an eye.
Even my ex-wife offered to phone him—Morgan. Her name is

Morgan. My father's, Irving. I say this in attempt to bring you
closer by that nominal bit—you, whoever you are "out there,"
Venusian in your distance from these people I love—you, reader.
If I told you that the night nurse is Arlene? Arlene
Bedoya. And I never did find out the name of her "strange
husband" "in Miami" "wit that batch" although I later learned
the batch's name was Topsy, so heard it correctly:
estranged. She hopes "to win me back his ol heart." I know

at shift's end, in the weak leaking out of Chicago's first
dirty light from the skin of the lake, she goes home and
runs her hands over the Christmas gifts she's wrapped for him
—it's only October—over and again, as if to build up some
electrical charge that might power her love clear to Florida. I know
I made of myself a present to my father in that same way, wanting
some volt to accrue that would heal—so, yes, I visited him,
I watched for a spark, I visited him repeatedly.

□ □ □

The last of his tasks. All dawn the sky more milky-gray
than a fish-innard condom. Now, though, sun
breaks through; and on a high plateau of comb-grass where the dew is
still a sticky kiss on everything, he picks one bead of it
up in a knotted stem and, with the patience of the poor-for-generations,
focuses sun through. Fire. From water. Winning the princess's
hand, and the princess's sweet cream-bodied breasts, and . . .
enough. Let them couple alone in a cloak of the Japanese night,

in love the whole length of their story. And Tony
and Sharon; and Karen and Danny-in-Drag; and the Wolkens . . .
in love their whole length. And then? And then, and then.
When Jimbo knocked at 4 a.m. his gut was on his tongue.
"We split up." *snap* "Like that." All over, entire cities, 4 A.M.,
the tiny bones of whole lengths breaking *snap, snap, snap* . . .
Now what to tell our Nipponese sweeties sporting their one
long fill'er-up night on the rice-white silks? And

Morgan, didn't we make our fire? From water,
from air, from the fur and the rind. From antimatter. Fire.
From the shine in the knob on the door at the very shimmybone-end
of the raw blue hallway of nothing. Didn't we
arson its planks? Baby, weren't the banks of the river Body
ablaze, their nerve-tip cattails torched? Baby, didn't we
kindle? Weren't we candescent fleshes? Didn't we burn?
Well, yes. And now here is its urn, and its ashes.

□ □ □

Even my ex-wife offered to phone him . . . One morning, a moment
before sun chutes through his window, I think of the serial
travel of language in "telephone"—the children's game. No matter
their exactitude in repetition, something like *my life is
one of plenty* transforms. The rhino Dürer did
became the rhino all of Europe did, in stages away
from that model, for over two centuries—a 200-year-long
flipbook of the fabulous. Scant changes departing from archetype

—so, evolution. Or film. Imagine a movie
in which each hundredth frame of the reel varies even only
slightly. Given infinity and an opening shot of Tara, we
might still achieve the whole of *Gone With the Wind* . . . Sun
enters, winnowed by blinds, and touches every bedside object,
touches the photo I've placed here—he's a young man,
younger than I am now, and holding me . . . And I whisper
to one, or maybe both, of these fathers of mine, *My wife has*

upped and left me. Now the sun is gilding
everything; along his cheek each stubble catches flame.
A crowd of pilgrims bearing candles. Angels burning
on the plain. In the *Sheet of 1,000 Buddhas* no
two are the same, not really. In one, the nimbus nearly
burnt-out like a bulb. In one, that circle of *satori*-glow
so inky it's a parka-hood. And a Buddha so faintly
stamped on the paper, he seems being eaten by light itself.

□ □ □

Pain sleeps around. Pain visits my father and tongues hot
damp fidelities in his ear, and yet I walk the ward and witness
pain hop body to body, sleazetramp, bedjumper,
anyone's for a night. So I was wrong. Pain isn't "insular," it's
held in common. Maybe that's true of joy as well; the village church
and town whore both are meeting-places, after all, I've heard
men speak about in terms of democratic entry even though
the time inside is of necessity a private one. But joy

is for another poem, or other part of this poem. I mean pain.
I mean the irreducible atom of hurt when Jimbo told Yvonne
about his lover we'd all take later to calling The Spider Woman
because of how he danced trapped at the sticky pit of her web . . . I see it
turning, silver, cold, in place
in the horrible center-of-gravity keeping Arlene Bedoya from rising
out of the flesh that remembers and into new flesh fresh
of experience. Brothers; Arlene and Jimbo are brothers, are sisters. One

night, hopeless, I walked miles under a moon like a bit of
mineral spar too small to save the smallest of anyone down here
from drowning in darkness. Walking, over to the lake.
And singing—keening, more like it. A song of soul-
puked-up-the-gullet. Walking, to the line where earth and wave
contended. Walking, alone. And not alone, not truly,
Tony, not ever, Jackie H., conceiving this, planning the stanzas,
walking the edge of everyone's divorce.

□ □ □

The fall shows rerun in summer. / Individual ragged
salmon return up the rungs, squeeze deep of the last of their own
full milt-sacs, shudder, and turn to single bloody-silver
muscles floating the current. And then? / An AM station cycles back
the goldies, and the new songs are the old songs anyway: heartbreak,
heartsublimity. And then? / The legends say Arthur will
return. And Quetzalcoatl, return. And the miracle-speaking
Messiah of the Jews. And then? And then. / My niece of all

of 2½ years, Lindsay Nichol, is driving the whole house fucking
nuts with her day's two new-learned words *supwise!* and *hostabul,*
running them endlessly in and out of her brain's maze
like white lab mice till the lessons are learned past doubt.
Wheh Gwampy? Grampy's sick—remember?—but
we'll let you talk on the phone. And later that evening, at his hostabul
bed, they'll loosen the tubes when the phone rings. Gwampy? Hewwo
supwise! And then? / October: the leaves,

their interior pyrrhic gold-reds. And then. The repetitions. How
they mean a separation. How they mean a tie. / Picasso:
how an ancient Dogon fertility dancer stares through the eyes
of his cubed Cannes bathing beauty. / Halley's comet: a comma
on fire—one of a series. / DNA. / And then? / And always
"and then." And the moon. Then no moon. / "One virtue
exists for the vastest mass of mankind:
Money."—this said by Theógnis, mid-sixth century B.C.

□ □ □

October: morning. Arlene Bedoya rehearsing her passionate Christmas
wrapping paper and ribbons. Here, I say my own one line,
in my own one mouth, I've never repeated out loud to this man but
aim at his body in silence, send in silence, like a sound wave
from a mute, through where his labyrinthine systems grip
and fail, down the grain of him and its every more-minuscule ripple.
I love you. Morgan's sent a card. He reads it, smiles. She's
x'ed a line of kiss-signs on it, my ex. So now I've been in both

their bodies, in my own way, for a small time, but no matter
whatever connection remains, must go on as and into
myself even longer. When I started this poem, I wanted to say
a true thing, and conclusive. But I see it's only another day
of charts and oxygen, fear and peripheral hope. Old
patients check out, new in. They're wheeling the many moaning
words of the text of our mortality from one ward to another,
bed to bed, like printing, like slugs of movable

type. And of the message Chunosuke Matsuyama
scratched on wood and gave, a last communication, to
the flux . . . ? What are the odds? What are the crazy ineffable units
of sun, of salt? In 1935, it washed up—over 150 years
later—on the beach outside a tiny Japanese fishing village. The
village of his birth. If I rewrite this poem or you reread it, you
out there in the Yonder (yes, reread it: please) leave that small note
of closure in. It's a heartening fact. And then some.

Pop. Cult. Crash Course

Elbee Novelty Company Inc.
1985

For I have seen Louie Berkie in his warehouse rows of plastic
Dog Poo, rubber chickens, Beagle-Puss glasses and snap cigarettes,
the boneyard and revival ward of 1947's Party Vomit,
Fool 'Em bon-bons, Squirting "Fountain" Pens and X-ray Specs,
while the whole 6th floor of the Calcasieu Building trembles
like the angels' own Joy Buzzer, at the metallic and bronchial hack
of the wooden nickel machine "and I print both sides" "and
orders come in from New Mexico even" "and charities half-price." And
the elevator of the Calcasieu Building smells of piss, of real human
piss, not Eau de Toilet "give-em-a-wiff!", but the compiled
untended accidents and sacrileges of 1947 to date, that can't be
bought or later laughed away, but must be only witnessed
after the fact, transparent uric-yellow ghosts,
as the cage wheezes open and Louie Berkie greets you in
his Pop-Out Eyes, "just look wherever you want, hey Rosie
give this guy a bag, just fill the bag, who wants these anyway,
when I die they can put a hundred thousand goddam
squirt carnations on my grave." For I have filled my bag.
For the matchbook snaps, and the chewing gum snaps,
and the dribble glass works like a wonder. And the employees of
the Elbee Novelty Company Inc. work wonders no less.
For the man without teeth stacks Chattering Teeth in what could be
Hieronymus Bosch's Walk-up School of Dentistry supply room,
and the boy without a work permit or English is filing bogus
permits—Fishing, Fucking, Bullshitting, Parking, Mooching—by
a personal system of color and width-of-animated-astonishment in
the eyes and leaping buttocks of the figures depicted thereon, and
Rosie—Rosie who hasn't saved a penny has tended these nickels
stamped with the logos of wholesale faucet distributors and furriers
since 1947, Rosie No-Last-Name, Our Lady By Now Of A Million
Wooden Bucks. And Louie Berkie can show you exploding
cigars all day and not tire. And Louie Berkie can light up his nose.
"Here look at the classic, the universal Palm Shocker, always good
for a *Ha!!*" And his real eyes light really up.
"We all need a gag" and "we all want guffaws" and "I live alone,
one thousand Suction Zulu Dancers, I like to make everyone happy but
tell me who the hell wants to inherit a wall of Suction Zulu Dancers?"
For dice can electrify. For fly-in-the-icecube won't

melt, fly or fail. And the street in front of the Calcasieu Building,
200-something Broadway, San Antonio Texas, smells like, yes and is,
the afternoon's true introduction to the Calcasieu Building elevator, and is
the Elbee Novelty Company Inc.'s world of Original Forms where the puddle
of vomit in front of Europe Deli and News is real and the scars
won't peel off and be folded away. "I started a clown, and then I woke up
one morning and said, 'Sell things, let everybody be a clown.'" And
the liver spots on Louie Berkie's hands will not unstick for slipping
back in a cellophane wrapper, nor his tremor come unplugged. "Hoo, I love
when the first twinkle shows in their eyes." For I have rummaged the
dust-&-clutter of sneezing powder, itching powder, Bird Doo in such quantity
a Jackson Pollock action mural pales in scope, and Snake-in-a-Can.
For Bald Wig, Bum Wig, Beatnik Wig and Bozo Wig are tête-à-tête
in emptiness forever. And in 1947 Louis Berkowitz was 30,
stocking shelves here for the first time, maybe running his hands
in grandeur down a catalogue's columns, Laffs-a-Lot's, the way somebody
else might turn in bed and for the first time
trace a naked spine. And lettering the street signs
for his 6th floor city of yuks—Adult Goods, Party Favors, Gags . . .
For I have filled my bag with Mouse-in-the-Camera, Fake-O bedbugs,
latex worms, The Forehead Faucet, limp forks, smoking spoons.
For Rosie will make change out of a tree all day and drink herself real
shitdrunk all real night. And this is the Louie Berkie Happyrama 1947
Calendar pinned to a wall. "And this is my sister. She
died. It happens. You know? It happens." And
this is the leatherette Turkish Harem Peepbook
"with the best snapper in the business." Louie Berkie is in the business,
is in the funny stuff business and I know well, for I have seen him
walking his rows in the darkness, talking funny talk to 38 years and thousands
of the loveliest best snappers, cocked in expectation,
wasted maybe, beautiful to the right eyes maybe, here on the 6th floor,
"I'm 68," "I only wanted some laughter should fill up
the silence, right? I know, I live alone. Here, shake my hand on it.
. . . *HA!!*"

Powers

Whizzer, The Top, Phantasmo . . . They come back sometimes,
now that my father comes back
sometimes. With their lightningbolts sewn
the size of dinner utensils across their chests, with their capes
rayed out, with their blue lamé boots. And he . . . ? It's
hazy, usually; he's a part of that haze. It talcs
his early morning stubble, it muffles the worry
love so often set like candles in his eyes. And: "Albie . . ." /then
that smile meant kindly, but also to say it came from some source
wiser than mine/ ". . . all this reading is fine. But there's a
real world." It wasn't The Streak. It wasn't Mistress Miracle.
With their antigravity belts, their bellcurve muscles.
Night. One lamp. While he read every scrap of fiscal scribble
that said the rent couldn't be met, and in the darkness
tried to fight that vague opponent with every poor
persuasive scrappy peddler's stratagem he had, I read
by flashlight under the covers: City Hall was being burgled
of its Gems of the World display, and Captain Invincible faced
a Mineral Ray (that already turned 2 bank guards and a porter
into clumsily-rendered crystalline statues) jauntily,
his wisecracks by themselves could make a "mobster" or
that dreaded gorillaish creature in a double-breasted suit,
a mobster's "goon," collapse in the ultimate cowardly self-exposure
of "crooks" and "scoundrels" everywhere. The Dynamo
could will himself into a wielder of electrical jolts, and even
invaders from Alpha-10 were vanquished. Smasheroo's
special power was fists "with the force of entire armies."
Flamegirl was . . . well, flames. And flying,
almost all of them, blazoned on sky—a banner, an imperative
above our muddling lunch-and-shrubbery days.
With their "secret identities": Spectral Boy, who looks like someone's
winter breath (and so can enter "criminal hideouts" through keyholes,
etc.) is "in reality" Matt Poindexter, polo-playing dandy;
The Silver Comet, whose speed is legendary and leaves
small silver smudges on the page as he near-invisibly zips by, is
ironically wheelchair-bound and Army-rejected
high school student and chemistry ace Lane Barker;
The Rocket Avenger parks cars; Celestia is a bosomy
ill-paid secretary. It could happen—couldn't it?—

to me: the thick clouds part as neat as prom-night hair
and a nacreous flask of Planet Nineteen's "wizard elixir" be
beamed down to my bedside: I would wake reciting
a Pledge Against Evil, and set to work designing whatever
emerald star or halo'd eye would be incised on my visor, it
could happen, right?—I wasn't Me but
an inchoate One of Them. With their Wave Transmitter Wristlets,
with their wands, their auras, their cowls. The Insect Master.
Blockbuster. Astro Man. Miss Mystery. Gold Bolt. Solaris . . .
They come back to me now, they ring the bedroom air sometimes
like midges at the one watt of my consciousness, and sleep
is entered with this faint token of sentinel benignity upon me.
Maybe because sleep also
isn't what my father called the "real world." And
he . . . ? Dead
now, with his stone, with his annual candle, my father is
also a fiction. And so he appears
with their right to appear, from the kingdom of the impossible,
he appears in their midst, with Doctor Justice,
The Genie, The Leopardess, Meteor Man . . . he steps out
from that powerpacked crowd, he's thrown his factory outlet jacket
sloppily over his shoulders, it's late, so dark now, and
he's worried about me. Someone may as well be. I'm
in pieces over some new vexation: hopeless in the drizzle,
perhaps, a flashlight clamped abobble in my mouth, and trying to find whatever
damage in the mysterious shrieks and greaseways of an engine
bucked me ditchside in the wee hours; or, with equal befuddlement,
staring damp-eyed at the equally damaged wants and generosities
awhirr in the human heart. And: "Albie . . ." /then that very
gentle yet censorious shake of the head/ " . . . how many times
have I told you? Be patient. Never force your tools or materials.
Don't give up." At moments like this, that his blood
pumps through me, his blood is half of what actually made me, seems
as wondrous as Bob Frank "deep in the jungles of Africa"
dying of fever and being saved by—positively
thriving on—a transfusion of mongoose blood.
This was in 1941, in USA Comics; Frank returned to New York
as the Whizzer—superfast, in an outfit
the yellow of mariners' slickers. And Triphammer.
Ghost King. The Scarlet Guardian. Eagleman. Magic Scarab. The Wraith.
With their domino masks or their gladiatorial helmets.
The Mighty Elasto. Lady Radiant. Space Devil. Reptile Boy.
With their various signs of legitimacy: their pharaonic rings,
atomic lariats, stun guns, mystic arrows, tridents, with

such amulets as hinge the Earth and Heavens into symbiotic grace.
The Invoker: I remember, he kept two planets at peace. And Hydro-Man:
could turn to water (a dubious strength, I always thought) and once
he conducted a current that fried some miscreant, so rescued
a willowy flibbertigibbet princess. And Panther Woman: her golden claws
and sinuous inky tail were all the good that (successfully) stood between
a scientist "bent on enslaving the world to his crazed whims" and
the populace of "Center City," the first place on his list. And
Whizzer . . . I remember, once, Whizzer was . . . I put down the page.
The knocking. The landlady. He was shaking
in front of her. She filled the door. He had to explain
the doctor cost extra money this month, and he worked all week
on double shifts, he really did, but this one time
we didn't have the rent, we'd be late, he was fighting back crying,
who'd never had to say such a thing before to such a person,
I remember: he said it straight to her face,
the one good pair of suit pants keeping its crease in the closet
cried but he didn't, the long day's wadded-up tissues cried out,
and the bar sign blinking pinkly across the street,
the horseshoes of dust that collect on the house slippers under the bed,
The Little Taxi That Hurried and *Scuffy the Tugboat,* that sorrily-stained
lame angelwing of an ironing board, the ashtrays and the aspirin,
everything yielded up its softness then,
the carpet was green and black, the light was ruthless,
his voice never broke and his gaze never shifted although
the universe did, because we would be one week late, there! he said it,
he said it clearly, to her and to everyone,
spent, and heroic.

The World Trade Center

Miss Cherry Harvest of 1954 is savvily bing-bedecked
in snug red mounds of endorsement. Miss Home Hardware
overflows a gray bikini-top (done as a wingnut). Miss
Asbestos Insulation. Miss Kosher Franks. The Aluminum
Siding Queen of 1957. "I was never so completely
cherished, or so much a dispensary of happiness, as that
night distributing candy samples and wearing the fabulous
sack that said REFINED, Miss Sugar Industry always wore . . . "
In jade: Miss Lawn Fertilizer, a weedy fringe
over her goodies. In gold: Miss Beer of the Year. "I was never
so debased. All night, this gross parade of paunchy gawkers
asking to eat my donuts, or punch the holes out
of my donuts, or use their cream in my donuts, or put their
nuts on my donuts. Thirty years later I hate those people
still. And donuts." Miss New Paper Goods
in marbled corrugation. The Bow-and-Arrow-Fair Queen.
Miss Kitchen Appliances waving like the Pope, though with
a greater sartorial splendor than the Pope's, from her silverized
pedestal at the heart of an 8-foot facsimile blender and
when it's on, she pirouettes in facsimile of its power and speed.
The Cupcake Girl. The Hog By-products Lady of 1962. We
need to love them. If every present moment is only a choice
some moment planted in the past made, then we need to love
these seeds of us if we're to love ourselves. Miss
Railroad Boxcars doing her choo-choo shuffle,
Miss Poultry, Miss Dry Ice. And little foil-petaled
nougat-and-marshmallow come-ons for the kiddies. One
free packet of cleanser. A complimentary photo of yourself
agog in the per-hour arms of Miss Pool-and-Patio Barbeque
while her court of attendant Charcoal Briquettes in their smokey hose
and baggy ash-like swimsuits dances in back. We
need to condemn them. This is the clownshow, this is the horribly
misshaped idea of sex's functions, and this
is the wedding of physical loveliness with commerce, we
contain as possibilities, let bloom sometimes and
need to root out. Miss Midwest Pharmaceuticals Co-op.
Need to refute. To look at us looking at Miss
Electric Handtools Festival looking at herself,
and gag. "I loved the attention, I loved making everyone feel

good, and nobody took it too seriously, it was fun just
like a mardi gras, and why not, I guess you can say,
well, I loved it." Miss Home Furnishings bouncing her bosomy
sponsorship of "Comfort *plus* Affordability" to and fro on the
bosomy couch. Miss Styrofoam. Miss Nuclear Power.
"I'd drag home dangling trains of plastic pretzels
off my fanny, so humiliating, and after a night of stinking drunk
tycoons and their yes-men downing slabs of sirloin and champagne
I'd open the door on my mother feeding on tea and breadcrusts and
I'd slam down my lousy day's wage." Miss Phone of the Future.
Miss Potato Crop of 1959. "A lot of care went into it,
all of the papier-mâché croissants and bagels they sewed on, and all
of the themesong lyrics, which I helped with" (sings:) "I'm the Bakery
Queeeeen with the tender lovin' oven" (now a faraway glazed look
in her eyes:) "I'll
never be that alive again." Miss American Plumbing. Miss
Sporting Goods. We must look at them closely, every
lipsticked mouth a beet-red butterfly quivering over hilly
fields of décolletage. The Lingerie and Sleepwear Queen.
Miss Fireproof Camping Gear. Miss Lumber Exposition. We
must look at them wholly, culture-wide, cross-time, like flowers
in speeded film, so many gauzy tutus bèing donned and doffed
a day—if these are flowers relegated to another age
by evolution, still we need to preserve their most exquisite sherbet pastels
and their greatest butchercolor striations. Vibrant
delegates of their mute, assigned constituency: wood paneling,
doorknobs, freestone peaches, tractor tires, picnicware.
Miss Pet Food. Miss Circus Equipment. Miss Pickle of
1957, 58, 59 and 60. And where are you now,
Miss-Pickle-handing-out-gherkin-slices, the welter
of seagreen spinach-and-celadon confetti long swept away, and where
are you now, Miss Carpet Shampooing Institute, now what
doting grandmama or business mafiosa have you been
borne to by the rising tide of that yesteryear's foamy bubbles?
I mean it. People die, and these traces remaining
pain us, Miss Furs, Miss Radio Home Repair—where
did your idling taxi finally breeze you afterwards, and
what became of that 10-year-old in the thick black glasses
watching you whisk grotesquely but ineffably away
until his father said "Albert it's late" then they left too
and what's become of the one in his grave and the other becoming
the age of the one, Miss Memory-Up-In-A-Puff,
Miss First-Wet-Kiss-With-Its-Glory-And-Shame, Miss
Lexicon-Of-Woe, Miss Poetry-Firing-Over-The-Skin, Miss Confusion,

Miss Needlepoint Maxims, Miss Funeral Shovel, Miss Semenburst,
Miss Everything, Miss Spider-Of-Blood-In-Its-Bodywide-Web.
We hate you. We're telling you now: we're ashamed,
Miss Amalgamated Canning Concerns, Miss Taxidermy, Miss
Soybean Dealers. Miss Generating Stations with the tiara
of flashing lightbulbs in your platinum hair. Miss Guilt.
Miss Undeniably Breathtaking Tenderness. Miss Knife-and-Gun.
We value you, with incredible passion. Miss Loosened Burnoose
in the Deepening Desert Sunset, Miss Tonsils, Miss Lesbian Love,
Miss Verdigris Glimmering Beautifully On A Hull Though No One Sees It,
Miss Guava Bushelboys of the Tropics, Miss Beef, we want you,
come nearer, be ours, Miss Manmade Fibers, Miss Avocado, Miss
Charge-Built-Up-About-A-Lightning-Rod-Like-A-Vigorous-
Sweetheart-Imagined-Around-The-Dildo, Miss Penance,
Miss Tallow, Miss Fossil, Miss Radium Technology, come
hither, where are you, what's happened to almost everyone
we know, do you remember us from that evening
in the fog we'd bring like intermittent patches of forgetfulness
for the rest of our lives and our seeking, tell us. Do you
miss us? Miss Us. Miss You.

The Quest for the Source of the Nile

They needed to know. They came, they suffered
swamps, bull rhinos, dysentery—Speke fell deaf
and blind—black fever (named from the phlegm), malaria,
tribal war, the worms in a stool like waxy gobbets of fat
in a headcheese, and a torn arm swaddled in calico
and cowpiss (which worked). They needed to know.
They needed to add that small blue comb of water
to their maps, and no irascible croc with power
to stop a hippo dead was going to stop their march.
They tramped past native huts for decades, for the source.
(In one, a chief and his youngest wife embrace. Their
ten year-old, the boy, is at the linen pull-to, listening: this
moaning is a mystery he can't explain, but something keeps him
unshakeably crouched. The Unknown. X. His Headwaters.)

□ □ □

There are places nearby without natural salt. The natives
pit-trap rats and suck the blood for salt, or trade
two measures of gold to a measure of salt
from occasional caravans. It's wonderful, salt. In one standard American
table grain are 10-to-the-16th sodium and chlorine atoms
—10 million billion. They grid themselves in a crystal order
more strict than a landscape of lamp posts in the best-laid city.
Think of walking into that grain, as out one night
through dark suburban blocks: past luminous
globe on globe, for miles, exactly. Think of being drawn
along the boulevards of atoms, of receding
with the atoms, past their logic. Someone, somewhere, pulling
back from this with fear salted over his body and someone,
elsewhere, venturing further. Think of needing to know.

□ □ □

—Not unlike walking the rule-edged ranks of hundreds
of thousands of falcon mummies, faience jar on jar until
they meet at the infinity-point, in the temple of Nectanébo II,
off the Nile. And here are the skies they're intended to fly through,
painted on the walls—the skies of Eternity, and
these long dark rows of jars become its merging lane. Confusing
death with forever is something dyed in our fibers from birth;
consider "dying" meaning "coming" in Elizabethan love verse.
When I've polled my friends of either gender about their
"first time," always—if it was good at all—a word like
"flying" or "falling" is used—"endlessly," "through space," "among
stars," then a great disappointment, and then an even greater
hunger for more. I mean for sex, for flesh, and I mean
for entering godhead, wherever beyond flesh it is.

□ □ □

My friend the writer Jim Magnuson is in Africa. My
friend Bob Lietz is stuck unemployed in the lusterless summer
of Bowling Green, Ohio. Even so, in his own way, he travels:
calls me: "Albert, listen, I've read we have this method now
arranging 7 lasers so they meet like a teepee frame and
when they do, they can slow an atom—we can train on an atom
and bring it toward absolute stasis." Maybe Bob's father is
there, if he's anywhere now; and mine, for that matter. I tell him
I'm reading we can test paternity cases now
down into the world of red-cell enzymes. Nothing
stops the ductile reach of our needing-to-know. I have
a photo of my father: I can see myself in his face. And a
photo, a skull from Kenya from 2½ million years ago: it
looks like a cave, and all of our fathers peeking from its sockets.

□ □ □

That morning, I'd caught them in bed. It was Sunday,
and maybe their special day of privacy and play, before
another week of laborious shlepping began. He rolled 1)
off his wife and 2) on his pants, in one rough, blushing
move and announced it was time (though I knew it was early)
to walk me over to Sunday School. The morning light was gritty
in his shaving talc in his neck-creases: I remember that.
And in school, I remember, the raisin-eyed daughter of Pharaoh
lifting pink pudge Baby Moses from his cradle the Nile
bore in its royal-blue hands, from reedy shadows into the public
touch of the sun. We all knew what happens ahead: the plagues,
the cloud of fire, tons of Yahweh-thunder and -glory. But
I was crazy for knowing what happened before: the place
a person comes from, upriver, where water first broke, the source.

□ □ □

Slitting cadavers—entering there like a puppeteer's hands
through stage drapes; parsing ever finer, if need be down
to a rigorous meat confetti—the abbot, in John Fuller's novel
Flying to Nowhere: trying, cut by cut, to discover the anatomical
home of the soul. I know, yes—it's "fiction." Someone might
say "only" fiction. And this is fact: the souls of the dead
return each year to the mountains of Michoacán as millions
of monarch butterflies—just ask anybody
bearing a baked clay thimble of sugar water, you'll see. And
was it true?: my father, arranged in a coffin.
Painted, folded, stretched. And was it true, as I'd remember
for years, I bent and saw down through the weave of him,
into a tiny room, empty now, and with an empty chair
and an open window and two white curtains fluttering like wings.

□ □ □

Bob Lietz is out walking. I know: the fussy
neighborhood blocks give way in a while, all of what Ohio
calls the sky meets what the Earth calls outer space.
Whatever nailheads studding a blackwall tire the stars are,
they're oracular as well, and filled with the mystical lizards,
hares, viziers, boars, androgynes and thorncrowned sages we place there.
He walks, he doesn't even have questions, but anyway waits
for an answer: some meteor shower clawmarking the dark,
satori, eureka, direction . . . I know, because I've walked that
walk. And after shitbugs sup Speke's open wounds and Baker
eats grass, the map may finally be etchinghatched triumphantly
with loci, but nothing stops walking like ours, or wanting.
"Of the sources of the Nile," wrote Herodotus, "no-one can give
account. It enters" moon gene mind mons embryo & dust "from parts beyond."

□ □ □

Jim Magnuson is in Africa. The air there is another planet
ghosts live on, *mbolozi;* for them *we're* hazy, passing
through the walls of their world. They change into leopards.
They gossip, there are millions of them, "whole perfectnumber," and
heaven hints mysterious things in our heads through their transparent
conductivity. A father died and a son living 7 villages distant
knew it—dropped to his knees in the field as if from a stone.
Jim Magnuson is a novelist, they often make up a character's
dreams for convenience. But this one, his, he swears is true:
he's back there, running under the sun (although it's night).
Lianas, he says, whipped his skin. Savannah grass slipped by.
He was frantic, looking for something, joyful and frightened,
symbolic—there for all of us. "Tell me the names of the gods,"
he was screaming. "Tell me the names of the gods!"

Qebehseneuf

William Petty in the seventeenth century attained considerable noto-
riety when he began to anatomize Anne Green, a murderess, and
found that she revived under his scalpel.

—Albion's Fatal Tree,
Douglas Hay

I want this poem to be that black
she saw.
       The peccary
roadkill-death made general,
made an indication of peccaryness
like an animal on a tavern sign,
that children are afraid to touch
in the lobby display of the Austin Nature Center. . . .
she looked that far
beyond reclamatory powers. If
she did "dress flash," all razz and sass,
to cheat them of another scabby doxie in rags gone
weeping to do "the air jig" at the Hanging Tree,
if she stepped in the cart with a wedding gown on
and "flipped a fullmoon arse" at the crowd
from out of her cloud of bridewhite satin and taffeta,
and took the rope singing, took it on arteries
winged out wide in singing,
                    she was an ashen satchel
of death on the table, her only other colors
a mustard-green and muddied plum in the shape
of a braid biting into her throat. You could feel
its hard and regular ridges . . .
               Now
a small boy's screaming. The guide asks why.
She bends to the haunch of the peccary
where he's wild-eyed with horror, and asks.
He knows she knows he's seen
a shock of excelsiorwork and taxidermist's carving
through a peeled patch, and *that* he can tell her.

But how can he say
near Chimney Hills is a giant revolving cowgirl
sign, for some motel, but broken, so
by night you can see her fluorescent
ribcage glowing.

□ □ □

An Indian medical text of the 15th century
discusses closing intestinal wounds by lining
black Bengali ants along the rupture. Really.
They clamp it together. Their bodies are snapped off
and the jaws remain, as ample sutures
that dissolve by the time the wound heals. But—why
think of it? There she is, so
small. And when she sleeps she's even smaller.
My mother. The tubes running into her. That,
and the language they use . . . ! "cut her open." "do a little
exploratory." Yes, and when the last ant vanished,
then the bowel could be coiled back into the abdomen and
sewn up. A way of thinking of her now
I can return from. So small. A sleeping pill
has vanquished her, a pill the size of a typed *o*. She
will float that dark all night and wake
to gulp a breath of living, once, then sink through ether
back to the dark. And the language they use . . . !
They'll "put her under." The boy at the peccary
fainted. And was roused by the rub of a warm cloth.
Now I'm going to think about her in her oncology sheets
by thinking of him. But—deeper,
as her darkness is deeper.

□ □ □

It was something like this
that Anne Green said: "Me mummy wor anged
fer er filch uf a barrister's quidpouch off is person
wot she coaxed wi er winkin an doveycoos
into a stoyt of ineebriation in is coach
OR SO THOY SAY, an me dud wor anged
the bleedin peabroyn fer is poachin
uf a wormy-eaded brace o doocks off a jodge's estate
OR SO THOY SAY, an me sis wor anged an me own
true luf, th idjit sot, wor anged
wi me poolin is legs to asten th end uf is sooferin, AN
OY by Gawd an Satan an evury sober Christian witness
wor anged—AN CAME BACK! (*a pause—the children
in the street are the only ones who will listen a third
or fourth or seventeenth time to her tale, but they
listen rapt, and her stagey pacing takes direct effect*)
O it wor dark. O it wor blacker n noyt, o
blacker n ink on a printers thomb, an me darlins
oy felt black as Death meself alriddy
standing onder th oistin tree wi me own pine coffin
alongmeside loyk a woyt woyt shadow, everthin wor so black!
Loyk oy wor lookin into a scuttle o coaldust,
broyt, an soft, an in it me mum and dud an sis
an rumtwit Arry isself who oy luffed so dear
was callin me COME ERE COME ERE COME ON IN
AN KISS US IN THIS ERE SWEET BLACK DUST when
uf a sudden it wor loyk a and ad snatched me op
an out an a voice saying This
ere lattle coal lump still gots a bit o waitin an
burnin to do. (*wink*) An
whan oy opened me oyes
oy foun a Surjun bleenkin
ployin wi me bubbies in a pooblic ployce!

□ □ □

Mother, the gut is the longest of us.
It's 30 feet. It's our gravity, dragging.

Weren't you always ahead of us? Parting the traffic?
Testing the waves at the beach?

I once saw a gull there soar from its offal
so easily—air, parting air.

And mother, without it you'll simply be
the closest of us to flying.

□ □ □

Tutankhamun's intestines
were folded in linen, then
set in a miniature mummiform coffin
"of beaten gold
inlaid with colored glass and carnelian."
On the inner lid, the goddess Selket is
traced in the gold with her wings spread, proclaiming,
in glyph script falling like rain about her,
Now I place my arms on that which is given to me:
Qebehseneuf, who is now within my protection.
—More traditionally,
the simple stone "canopic jar" was used.
And here, the lid was carved
as the hawk-headed god and spirit-of-the-intestines
Qebehseneuf, and there might not even be an inscription.
Even so, his guardian beak is sharp and,
always, the worker who fashioned him has placed the eyes
in focus on a plane that we can only say
extends itself into Eternity.

□ □ □

Rotogravure. Lorgnette. Dagnabbit.
Some words truly die. But others . . .
Anne Green may have been like that: grabbed
last-minute out of her final blackflamed burning;
given second breath. She might be,
as these words are . . . quaint. "Maw, lookee!
Thir goes th Crazy lady!" "Leave er be,
poor thing wot promynods oldin conversoytion
wi erself." *Alembic. Roustabout. Phlogiston.*
O'er. In a conversation on poetics,
Galway Kinnell has talked of the singular pleasure
of salvaging junkheap words, of tuning them
lubed and ahum in new vehicles. *Mizzling,*
he uses, *stillic, droozed, bast, damozel, biestings*
—words be-aura'ed with the ancient power of having touched
the fossil possibility inside themselves,
considered it, then turned and taken
one last fullfleshed clarionhood on a living tongue.
She might be, as these words are . . . charged.
Phlebotomist. Escutcheon. Swain.
The Lazarus Lady who entered that unrefusable black of the pit
and refused it. "Maw . . ." "Hush! Lissen wot she be sayin."
Oracle Lady. Shaman Lady.
Black of the beetle, black of an ancestor's eyesockets.
Halcyon.
        Trilby.
                Cameleopard.
Lady who came back o'er.
Mugwumpery.
                Ectoplasm.
                        Pooch.
                                Scram.

□ □ □

Mother, the skin is the least of us.
The rest, the most, has never been touched by light.

And it will be all right. But first you need to pilgrimage
boustrophedon through your own gut-dark.

And it will hurt. (I couldn't lie.)
The form of it may say rape, say death.

It isn't enough you're on your knees.
We want you on your back.

The grass the blanket the . . .
Livia was four—remember? We
picnicked in Humboldt Park and a group
of older girls asked if Livia could "go to the water"
with them (meaning the swimming pool all afternoon)
and you said yes, sure (meaning the drinking fountain)
—remember? And three hours later there you were
in a cop car cruising all the leafy bylanes and screaming
you'd kill yourself if you didn't find her, the cop
saying lady now lady, then Livia stalking calmly
up to the cop announcing she'd learned to swim

                                    —which
over the years has taken on the lustrous-verdigris surface
of myth.

        These sheets; the nurses' chalky uniforms;
the patients' pale faces (all are calla lilies
centered on pillows) . . . White. Such white. Like living
in an aspirin. White, and day and night an artificial
regimen of visits, and everything, time included,
dissolving . . . You young again. Livia four: Me
squeezing the bark off a tree to study its grubs and
sun is on my cheek in a wedge as heavy and gold and
overhot as a slice of doublecheese pizza from Vito's
where Daddy's going to meet us. Your husband,
alive. Of course, alive, how crazy, 1956, and how come
Livia's not back yet with the girls, and light and
chlorophyll all over throwing soft aquarium
shadows on your own soft skin . . .

                          Now 30
years later, what is it
except the words we remember it in? The words
are everything, Mother.

                The words we save
are the words we save everything else in.

                      Really
what do we fear in looking at each other tonight
if not that every word we've said
so urgently between us all our lives
will herd at the edge of the memory record, stare
a moment into cloudiness, then step off . . .

                        love
being foreplay for loss.

☐ ☐ ☐

In a friend's friend's house, I've seen a vast
and gaudy collection of whiskey decanters;
a hula girl, a golfer, a kilted and bagpiped Scot,
a circus clown, an aeronaut, an alpine yodeler . . .
"And here," he said and winked, "we keep our spirits."

□

And here's the baboon-head canopic jar (the lungs).
And here's the jackal-head canopic jar (the stomach).
And here, a jar for grace (a mountain ibex).
And here, a jar for the brain (a dragonfly convoluting the air).
Or here, the mind (a dragonfly shadow).

□

Dark. A few pills
circling in your system for a clock.
How strange, in this city of windowledge pigeons and sparrows,
to be in the world of Qebehseneuf the hawk,
that spirit, your totem, night's lid.

□ □ □

And this is what we cherish: words
with one foot over the precipice,
called back
              to bodies again. In some
Medieval Hebrew manuscripts, the text
is done so finely, with such supple twists, as to be given
entirely over to forming the bodies of human beings,
beasts, and birds . . .
              A single "paragraph" might draw
the picture of two grass-appraising oxen, a parrot their
same size, fish, a huge central tree with a husband and wife
enjoying a supper under its reach, each leaf a word, each feather,
scale, flex of flesh . . .
              The whole of Creation, literally
from language, as it was "In the beginning . . . The Lord
said 'Let there be . . .'"
              Now what does He think
of a hospital, Mother? All of these bodies,
seen from His height, bent by the needs of their hundred
individual easings. What word
are we part of? *Tenderness. Torture.* A woman asleep,
and a man with his head in his hands like a flashlight
shining on her all night, afraid if it blinks off once . . .
                                        At
least we're still in His dictionary. An early 14th century Bible
from Germany speaks of a "great fish" and this text comprises
Jonah being heaved from the jaws of a whaleish thing.
How long he'd been lost in pain in that gut!
In darkness unimaginable! And here he is,
arms open in wonder, as if the creature is
comicbook-like speaking him
into the light of the page.

□ □ □

It was something like this
that Anne Green said (in translation): "I touched it.
I was there, I wore Death's black chemise.
Death took me partying. I swigged black hootch.
(The tongue has 10,000 buds and not one burned.)
I danced. I danced the black shimmy.
I shot black craps. The dice are black
and their markings are equally black. (Nobody wins.)
I rode in Death's luxury Caddie: mobster-black,
with monster fins and a one-way meter. Oh
children, listen: I was in Death's library. There
is only one entry in Death's thesaurus, "black," and then
a thousand thousand synonyms. Death's own
bed is black, and Death's lubricants black, and Death's sex
is a black prosthetic penetrating blackness. Listen,
oh children of mine: when Death was sleeping I
went for a walk on Death's black estate.
I undid the black deadbolt and slipped out alone.
The sky was like black acetate. The black grass sighed.
And something . . . Who knows what? But something . . .
Or how or why? But this: I heard my name being called
far off, *Anne Greeeeen,* or someone, maybe one of you,
but someone, saying *Mother.* Simply: *Mother.* Fastened,
strapped black in a black seat bolted black to the deck / some
marlin yanked me out and over
the waters, it hurt, I must have blacked out, I flew, and when
I opened my eyes light stung inside me like a white whip of salt.

□ □ □

da Vinci played a joke.
In Rome. The court of the Medicis.
Fancy schmancy. All the dinner guests
with ziggurats of painted snails and candied goose brains,
that kind of thing. What Leonardo did: he
inflated the entrails of a large ram with a bellows,
and from around a corner he launched those by-now
overballooning intestines floating
blimpwise into the room
                         —Why think of it now? Bengali ants . . .
Why say it? Eviscera spiraled by hand
like boat rope into their proper Egyptian ceramic . . .
And she's so delicate now, I think my touching her direct
could break her. So I need these gloves.
I need facts
returned from where she's a guest tonight
in the realm of the uttermost, returned but
in bearable form.
                    Or you might
or I might break.

□ □ □

This morning. And its whetstone dazzle.
Even through the shade of this immensely full-bouffant Chicago elm,
such light . . . its
edge could sharpen surgical blades.
They'll be shaving her now . . . So bright . . .
                                        Qebehseneuf,
hawk-god, guardian, weight it darker, a little, bring
the ageless rind of blackness I've seen smiling
in the mouth of your jar. A little. A hypo's worth.
A shot of inoculate
blackness up a vein, no more.
The band of black that blanks the skies each night and some nights
says, in the whisper-rush of roaches, in the oilblots under parked cars, it
refuses to yield, and
yet it yields. That blackness. Bring it. Be with me.
Take my affidavit. Listen: I pledge my pulse.
Attend her. Be gentle. They snug their handsize
ether-mask against the mouth and nose, and then it's endless
floatingfloating the anthracite-black backwash of the brain
until a person is revived; if. And Qebehseneuf,
see that she is. Reprieve her. Agitate for archangelic and
gubernatorial pardon. Black: Houdini's-top-hat-black: the flowers
disappear but the point is, pop back
later umpteenfold. Perform that magic. Saw and rebuild her. Pass that
inky fifth of blackberry brandy out, until she passes out,
and be there when she comes-to. Hawk-god, listen:
I'm just me. I try to write these poems, be middling decent
with a lady, not add overmuch malarkey to the thickening
slick of it filming this planet—for me it's enough
to enter another day. But you can enter rooms through walls,
you're a god, can enter through the protein of a body,
ride the hemoglobin, be there. Qebehseneuf:
be there. See the honest justice done. The first
incision now . . . This meat doll, on their slab . . . Be
in communion. Show your shape. Prescribe a draft of black
regurgitant. *Take two black every black.* Be her bannister.
Ready her, steady her, black a rhizome thrives in. That
rebounding black Anne Green saw, dozed in, rose from
cockadoodling with her noosed voice; and the black some words
return from, saved by maybe just a few
such uses as this: *Cahoots. Peruke. Hotdiggity.*
Potentate. Flummoxed. Tootsies. Imbroglio. Cuirass. Suzerainty.
I'm just me in the sun,
just me in the threshing of dust and light,

the deckled depositions of high tide over the shale,
the way the cosmos beats us like a good pimp
so no bruises show and then we shake back out to the street
and work for it, here in the sweetness
at the bullseye of pleasureful sex, and with whatever
rabbinical wisdom in our blood is mumbling
holiness and prohibitions, me in the morning,
me a halfass pinball-play in the maze of Chicago traffic,
walking, talking to an ancient Egyptian
idea of things, and a word even older,
as if she might hearken
and come to me as she always did when I needed her,
        me in the root of it,
        out in the weather.
          Please.

Mother.

☐ ☐ ☐

The kids are filing out of the Austin Nature Center.
"Whass that?"—one points.

The building's front is total glass. And the woman says,
"Small birds might crash here and die.

So these are the shapes of hawks
we put up cut from black paper.

A bird gets close enough, it spots the black hawks,
and it wheels right back where it came from."

Collecting: *an essay*
for Barbara & David Clewell

In the "fuckee bars" of that Oriental city, floor girls
sweep up after the sets with brooms maneuvered by their
beautifully bamboo and nearly hairless you-know-whats,
says Brady. And Brady says the great cathedrals of Europe are
easily rivaled by the architecture of waterfalls that yearly
freeze in the northern passes: minerals from the rock
have dyed those crystalline buttresses, domes, and rose windows
beatitude's colors, orchids and peacocks the lackluster
saints of stone would trade their longevity for—says
Brady. Brady's been a first-rank courier, the world

his office. One day a timelocked lacquer box of diamonds
to Nepal. Again, a set of "security-sensitive" directives
to a pair of silent bison-shouldered sunglassed "contact
deputies" in the sunken gardens of Rome. And the Company
pays for rests between: a week at the black-sand beach where
Brady looks like a pearl shrimp curled on a damp dune of caviar
(where, he says, he diddley-deed with an incognito countess and her
sweetcream-bosomed femme de chambre)—or once a series
of lectures on "Postmodernist Cuisine" at the Sorbonne. Collecting
is passion; these are some of the stories in Brady's album. Here,

today at the West End Weekly Flea, the pleasure is seeing
that same delight in acquisitions's intimate details settle to, and fit,
a stamp (one savvy haggler, 10, is zeroing in on a coveted
Smokey the Bear first-day-of-issue envelope showing
the bruin's gently admonishing visage staring ghostly
from a teal-blue fog) or one of the early 19th century butter molds
this woman with the beaky nose and moleskin collar seeks
and stores and knows by pattern better than most of us
know our own birthmarked skin: palmettoes, looped ivy,
webbing, escutcheony pineapples, cockatoos, rings-in-rings . . . I've seen

Babs bop down the pea gravel aisles in quest of fifties ceramics
with avidity that said by study and awe her very
red blood cells had taken on the vaguely amoebaish/boomerang
look of those wares; and Dave upscrutinizing snaggled cairns
of curios (bisque flappers and their beaus, time-rainbowed
bottles, scrimshaw humidors, a family of tux-and-top-hat
ducks whose scarlet derrieres are flower pots . . .) in search
of flying saucerania: everything from books of first-hand sightings
to those ashtrays (only squintily reminiscent of some Mother Ship)
he seizes with such discoverer's joy he looks more

otherworldly, whooping, beaming, than his Moonmen finally might.
I use their real names, and these are friends of mine. And I
belabor that because of the others, sharpster
sharkeye-guys and eel-ladies, you'll see slinking those same
democratic rows of bakelite mermaid pins and snuff tins but
with oozy markup and resale charging their hearts—which
is the spark of a battery different from love's, completely.
Babs, however, wouldn't merchandize one crappy plastic nut tray
in the pinch-waisted shape of a hula cutie, once her eye
has cherished it and fastened it connubially

near a zoot-suited spaceman of Dave's. She
renews the inflatable lobster, pig and bee; he keeps the working
1940's windup jug band working. So these objects
are the nuclei in a body of viable love. The rubber
Paddy the Penguin figurine, the poodle lamps, the loosely
oviform goldspecked aqua-trim formica end tables . . . "Albert,
if you ever see a near-mint Paddy the Penguin set of coasters . . ." or
posters or toasters or whateverthehell—they're
collecting. They're bricking their love in safe. They're
whipping themselves exquisitely toward completion. Mo,

the Mickey King of St. Louis, once ushered me upstairs from the shop
to his exemplary sanctum—everywhere, rare avatars of
the Mouse: as lavishly stashed as Vatican treasures, were
the 1935 Mickey and Minnie "play-me piano," the legendary
target game with the classic "pie-eyed" Mickey cheerfully bearing
the circle with 1000 points, of course the entire Mickey
circus train with prank-playing anthroanimal entourage,
et-endlessly-cetera, saved from time's indiscriminate ferret teeth,
display-cased as if the fate of the cosmos always rested on one
human being's accepting one task with devotion. For me, those

were the Judith Months: I wanted love conducting
efficaciously between two cities so damn much, my psyche
must have been raised in raffia-texture rashes of
hope and effort. Every day was only good material
for a letter to her, every night was overlaying her face
on the bodies of whackoff fancies—trying, as if Eros were
a god who might be wheedled by endurance.
I see now it couldn't flower—that takes soil more
than air. But then, those months, I thought that I could live on air
if she'd write back. And Mo's whole shelfdom told me

people's souls are said by their private devices.
What, doesn't matter—it's how. Whatever rich
collecting I did of that woman in my dreams, I do think
however I did it was right, and signaled something
of consummate care—she'd say the same of herself
and I'd let her. Yes, and so somebody's rummaging
turn-of-the-century ice cream scoops, and somebody Edison
patented gramophone cylinders, and somebody each intact Buck
Rogers raygun and an arsenal of ripoff zip- and zowie-
guns competitors peddled by thousands. I know: "you

can't take it with you." Not one pissant inch of pharaonic lapis
has, so far as we know, materialized amid the Eternal
Lotus Fields there on the Other Side. The tomb is no transport dock.
But sometimes I see this: I'm 7, up late with a cough and
playing in the basement, in the murkily aquarium-like light
sliding off of the battered pea-green office files. My father,
Old Man of a Hundred Woes and Integrities, is groaning. He's put
in another 12 heel-depleting hours hefting his records-book up
the back porch stairs of Cicero, Illinois—for pennies, sweating
cheap-valise insurance shlep that he is, collecting,

collecting. For Metropolitan Life—collecting. And
now that 10 p.m. should see him upstairs, healed in Fannie's arms of
everything deplorable about pitching a company line while dealing
honestly with clients, Mrs.-Koszhkie-of-the-one-eye,
Mr.-Blood-in-his-Handkerchiefopolous . . . here my
father is, math-addled, needing to get the day's
sums straight, and they won't, and the stinking rent and grocery
angst is on him. How I wish now I'd looked up
from coloring Mickey and Donald strictly inside the lines, and
known enough to tell him: even though the columns didn't, something

added up—it was (more, even than numbers)
what counted. Do we ever see that at 7?—how love can be
spoken although in disguise. At 37 I was standing
at his graveside with the mourner's *kaddish* standing
in its many black boots on my tongue. The Hebrew means
the Earth and Heavens should accept their respective percentage
of what his total was at last. And now at last
the living could say their love without embarrassment, nakedly.
(Judith, why can't we ever learn from such moments?) And
the rabbi said, in his words, this—which I give you now in mine:

"At the Gates a man shall be opened and his contents weighed.
Below, the wife she weepeth, and the son he stumbleth
clenched-up through the ritual farewells, yet above,
at the Gates, there is no shadow, for there is no solid object
anywhere to hinder light, and in such light a man is
valued by the being he bears and is, and so with Irving; and
it shall all be canceled stamps, and it shall all be
molded butter, and we shall all be couriers, hearken
to this, no not for caskets of jewels, and not fiestaware, but
a man is a message and we shall all be couriers, verily,

I say unto you: at the end, all of us—couriers."